OLD TESTAMENT THEOLOGY:

Basic Issues in the Current Debate

OLD TESTAMENT THEOLOGY:

Basic Issues in the Current Debate

by

GERHARD F. HASEL

WILLIAM B. EERDMANS PUBLISHING COMPANY

Grand Rapids, Michigan

Printed in the United States of America

Contents

Abbreviations

AUSS   Andrews University Seminary Studies
CBQ   Catholic Biblical Quarterly
EOTH   *Essays on Old Testament Hermeneutics*, ed. Claus Westermann (Richmond, Va., 1963)
EvTh   Evangelische Theologie
FRLANT   Forschungen zur Religion und Literatur des Alten und Neuen Testaments
IDB   *Interpreter's Dictionary of the Bible* (Nashville, 1962)
JBL   Journal of Biblical Literature
OaG   *Offenbarung als Geschichte*, ed. W. Pannenberg (2nd ed.; Göttingen, 1963)
OTCF   *The Old Testament and Christian Faith*, ed. B. W. Anderson (New York, 1963)
OTT   G. von Rad, *Old Testament Theology* (2 vols.; New York, 1962, 1966)
RScPhTh   Revue des Sciences Philosophiques et Théologiques
SBT   Studies in Biblical Theology
TAT   G. von Rad, *Theologie des Alten Testaments* (5th ed.; München, 1966)
ThLZ   Theologische Literaturzeitung
ThZ   Theologische Zeitschrift
TOT   W. Eichrodt, *Theology of the Old Testament* (2 vols.; Philadelphia, 1961, 1965)
VT   Vetus Testamentum
WMANT   Wissenschaftliche Monographien zum Alten und Neuen Testament
ZAW   Zeitschrift für die alttestamentliche Wissenschaft
ZThK   Zeitschrift für Theologie und Kirche

Introduction

Old Testament theology today is undeniably in crisis. Recent monographs and articles by European and American scholars[1] show that the fundamental issues and crucial questions are presently undecided and matters of intense debate. Though it is centuries old, OT theology is now uncertain of its true identity.

George Ernest Wright tells us in *The OT and Theology* (New York, 1969) that he has now changed and "must side with Eichrodt . . ." (p. 62). Earlier, in his well-known study *God Who Acts: Biblical Theology as Recital* (*SBT*, 8; London, 1952), he found himself close to the theological views of Gerhard von Rad with regard to the question of what constitutes OT theology.[2] The French theologian Edmond Jacob, on the other hand, has re-entered the ongoing discussion about the nature, function, and method of OT theology in his most recent contribution *Grundfragen alttestamentlicher Theologie* (Stuttgart, 1970), in which he further undergirds and defends his own position.[3] The same is true of the Dutch scholar Th. C. Vriezen. His thoroughly revised and expanded second English edition of *An Outline of OT Theology* (Newton, Mass., 1970)[4] exhibits a new em-

[1] See Supplementary Bibliography, pp. 97-98.

[2] *The OT and Theology*, pp. 61f. Note also Wright's essays "Reflections Concerning OT Theology," *Studia Biblica et Semitica. Festschrift Th. C. Vriezen* (Wageningen, 1966), pp. 376-388; and "Historical Knowledge and Revelation," in *Translating and Understanding the OT. Essays in Honor of Herbert G. May*, ed. H. T. Frank and W. L. Reed (New York, 1970), pp. 279-303.

[3] The new French edition of *Théologie de l'AT* (2nd ed.; Neuchâtel, 1968) deals in the preface also with the problems here under discussion. Two recent articles by Jacob are also very pertinent, "Possibilitiés et limites d'une théologie biblique," *Revue d'Histoire et de Philosophie Religieuses*, 46 (1966), 116-130; and "La théologie de l'AT," *Ephemerides theologicae lovanienses*, 44 (1969), 420-432.

[4] The 2nd English ed. is based upon the 3rd Dutch ed. of 1966, inclusive, however, of additions from the literature published after 1966.

phasis in regard to the communion concept. B. S. Childs has presented his penetrating and daring monograph *Biblical Theology in Crisis* (1970) in which he reports on the substance, achievements, and failures of the so-called Biblical Theology Movement in the United States, which is said to have reached its "end" and "demise."[5] He also proposes a new methodology for engaging in a "new Biblical Theology."[6] The European counterpart to the monograph by Childs comes from the pen of the German theologian Hans-Joachim Kraus, whose *Die Biblische Theologie. Ihre Geschichte und Problematik* (1970) is mainly concerned with the European history of the discipline since 1770.[7] This indispensable tome focuses at length on problems crucial to the discipline of OT theology (pp. 307-395).

These major contributions in monograph form indicate that the debate concerning the nature, function, method, and shape of OT theology continues unabated. It is not wrong to say at the outset that the discipline as a whole continues to remain in a state of flux. No general consensus in one direction or another has been reached. To the contrary, recent developments have led to a situation that is more complex than before. In view of these recent trends one can indeed speak of a "crisis" in OT theology in particular and in Biblical

[5] The exact date for the "end" of the Biblical Theology Movement as a dominant force in American theology is supposedly May 1963, the date of the publication of J. A. T. Robinson's *Honest to God;* so B. S. Childs, *Biblical Theology in Crisis* (Philadelphia, 1970), pp. 85, 91. See the reviews and critiques by M. Barth, "Whither Biblical Theology," *Interpretation,* 25/3 (July, 1971), 350-354, and Gerhard F. Hasel, *AUSS,* 10 (1972), 179-183.

[6] See here especially chs. 5 and 6 entitled "The Need for a New Biblical Theology" and "The Shape of a New Biblical Theology" in Childs, pp. 91-96, 97-122.

[7] It is surprising that Kraus mentions in only a few instances names of Anglo-Saxon scholars (pp. 2, 4, 5, 334, 336, 344, 373f.). Though he covers in greater detail much of what R. C. Dentan has covered (see Bibliography), he apparently does not even once refer to the latter's study.

theology in general.[8] It is necessary for each responsible exegete and theologian to continue to probe into the basic issues that determine the character of OT and Biblical theology, that give it new and meaningful direction, because what is at stake is not only the survival of a discipline but something that is crucial and decisive for the direction the Church — and through it men — may pursue in the quest for meaning in life.

In a presentation of the kind undertaken here we are able only to touch upon what to the present writer are major unresolved problems. It is our aim to focus on these crucial issues which are at the center of the fundamental problems in order to present the major current trends, and to build upon this discussion our own proposals for doing OT theology.

---

[8] Childs is the first one who uses the term "crisis" in a title. He is not, however, the first to employ this term with reference to either OT or NT theology. Among others we may refer to J. Hempel, "Alttestamentliche Theologie in protestantischer Sicht heute," *Bibliotheca Orientalis*, 15 (1958), 206ff.

I. The Question of Methodology

The fundamental question of methodology is one that encompasses a cluster of basic issues, and on which Biblical theologians have not succeeded in moving toward a single direction. Five clearly distinguishable major methods for doing OT theology are in vogue today. Yet not all these methods are mutually exclusive; although each theologian approaches OT theology mainly on the basis of one particular methodology, he may at the same time use also a complementary method. This fact makes the assigning of individual theologians as proponents of certain methods at times difficult. We have attempted to place the particular theologians that employ a multiple methodology under those methods that are most typical of their work or in the development of which they have made a special contribution.

A. *The Descriptive Method.* The descriptive method in the tradition of Gabler-Wrede-Stendahl[1] has its pro-

---

[1] Johann Philipp Gabler's inaugural lecture "Oratio de iusto discrimine theologiae biblicae et dogmaticae, regundisque recte utriusque finibus," delivered at the University of Altdorf, March 30, 1787, marked the beginning of a new phase in the study of Biblical theology through its claim that "Biblical theology is historical in character [*e genere historico*] in that it sets forth what sacred writers thought about divine matters . . . ." (in *Gableri Opuscula Academica II* [1931], pp. 183f.). Cf. R. Smend, "J. Ph. Gablers Begründung der biblischen Theologie," *EvTh*, 22 (1962), 345ff. Wilhelm Wrede's programmatic essay *Über Aufgabe und Methode der sogenannten Neutestamentlichen Theologie* (Göttingen, 1897), p. 8, emphasizes again the "strictly historical character" of NT (Biblical) theology. The penetrating and influential article of Krister Stendahl, "Biblical Theology, Contemporary," in *IDB*, I, 418-432, followed by his paper "Method in the Study of Biblical Theology," in *The Bible in Modern Scholarship*, ed. J. Philip Hyatt (Nashville, 1965), pp. 196-209, presents arguments for the rigorous distinction between "what it meant" and "what it means."

ponents to the present day in E. Jacob,[2] G. E. Wright,[3] P. Wernberg-Möller,[4] P. S. Watson[5] among others. The Biblical theologian is said to have to place his attention on describing "what the text meant" and not "what it means," to use Stendahl's distinctions.[6] The progress of Biblical theology is dependent upon a rigorous application of this distinction,[7] which is to be understood as a "wedge"[8] that separates once and for all the descriptive approach to the Bible from the normative approach of the systematic theologian, whose task it is to translate its meaning for the present. The latter task, "what it

[2] E. Jacob, *Theology of the OT* (London, 1958), p. 31, states that OT theology is a "strictly historical subject." In a somewhat more cautious tone he maintains recently that no method may claim absolute priority over another, because a theology is always *"unterwegs" (Grundfragen alttestamentlicher Theologie*, p. 17) and for doing OT theology there are various ways open (p. 16). At the same time he maintains that a theology of the OT has the task of presenting or expressing what is present in the OT itself (p. 14).

[3] Wright, *God Who Acts*, pp. 37f., expresses at length that he believes Biblical theology to be a "historical discipline" which is best described as a "theology of recital, in which man confesses his faith by reciting the formative events of his history as the redemptive handiwork of God." The later Wright, who now feels closer to Eichrodt than von Rad, holds on to the notion that Biblical theology is a "descriptive discipline." See G. E. Wright, "Biblical Archaeology Today," in *New Directions in Biblical Archaeology*, ed. D. N. Freedman and J. C. Greenfield (New York, 1969), p. 159.

[4] Wernberg-Möller (see Bibliography), p. 29, argues for a "descriptive, disinterested theology."

[5] "The Nature and Function of Biblical Theology," *Expository Times*, 73 (1962), 200: "As a scientific discipline, Biblical theology has a purely descriptive task. . . ." See the critique by H. Cunliffe-Jones, "The 'Truth' of the Bible," *Expository Times*, 73 (1962), 287.

[6] *IDB*, I, 419.

[7] Here Stendahl follows the position of the contributors from Uppsala University of the volume *The Root of the Vine: Essays in Biblical Theology*, ed. A. Fridrichsen (London, 1953), who agree that Biblical theology is primarily a historical and descriptive task to be distinguished from later normative reflections.

[8] Childs, *Biblical Theology in Crisis*, p. 79, objects to the dichotomy reaffirmed by Stendahl on the basis that it drives a "wedge between the Biblical and theological disciplines" which the Biblical Theology Movement sought to remove.

means" for today, is not to be considered a proper part of the strictly historical descriptive method.

B. S. Childs[9] objects against the descriptive method on account of its limiting nature. The descriptive task cannot be seen as a neutral stage leading to later genuine theological interpretation. The text, says Childs, is "a witness beyond itself to the divine purpose of God." There must be "the movement from the level of the witness to the reality itself."[10] Stendahl concedes that the descriptive task is "able to describe scriptural texts as aiming beyond themselves, . . . in their intention and their function through the ages...."[11] But Stendahl denies that the explication of this reality is a part of the task of the Biblical theologian. Childs, however, insists that "what the text 'meant' is determined in large measure by its relation to the one to whom it is directed." He argues that "when seen from the context of the canon both the question of what the text meant and what it means are inseparably linked and both belong to the task of the interpretation of the Bible as Scripture."[12] A. Dulles makes a similar point when he speaks of the "uneasiness at the radical separation . . . between what the Bible meant and what it means." Whereas Stendahl gives normative value to the task of what the Bible means, Dulles maintains that normative value must be given also to what the Bible meant. If this is the case, then Stendahl's dichotomy is seriously impaired because "the possibility of an 'objective' or non-committed descriptive approach, and thus . . . one of the most attractive features of

9 "Interpretation in Faith: The Theological Responsibility of an OT Commentary," *Interpretation,* 18 (1964), 432-449.

10 Pp. 437, 440, 444.

11 *The Bible in Modern Scholarship,* p. 203 n. 13.

12 *Biblical Theology in Crisis,* p. 141.

Stendahl's position" is done away with.[13] Similar points are made by R. A. F. MacKenzie, C. Spicq, and R. de Vaux.[14]

It may be that we need to be reminded by O. Eissfeldt that "auf geschichtlichem Wege vermögen wir nicht zum Wesen der alttestamentlichen Religion vordringen."[15] How can the non-normative descriptive method with its limiting historical emphasis lead us to the totality of the theological reality contained in the text? By definition and presupposition the descriptive historical method is limited to such an extent that the total theological reality of the text does not come fully to expression. Does Biblical theology need to be restricted to be nothing more than a "first chapter" of historical theology? If Biblical theology has also normative value on the basis of the recognition that what the Bible meant is normative in itself, then would it not be expected that Biblical theology must engage in more than just describing what the Biblical texts meant? Biblical theology is not aiming to take the place of or

13 "Response to Krister Stendahl's Method in the Study of Biblical Theology," *The Bible in Modern Scholarship*, pp. 210f. Stendahl, of course, maintains that there is no "absolute objectivity" to be had (*IDB*, I, 422; *The Bible in Modern Scholarship*, p. 202). He is completely right in emphasizing that the relativity of human objectivity does not give us an excuse to "excel in bias," but neither, we insist, does it give us the possibility of doing purely descriptive work.

14 R. A. F. MacKenzie, "The Concept of Biblical Theology," *Theology Today*, 4 (1956), 131-135, esp. 134: "Coldly scientific—in the sense of rationalistic—objectivity is quite incapable of even perceiving, let alone exploiting, the religious values of Scripture. There must be first the commitment, the recognition by faith of the divine origin and authority of the book, then the believer can properly and profitably apply all the most conscientious techniques of the subordinate sciences, without in the least infringing on their due autonomy or being disloyal to the scientific ideal." C. Spicq as quoted in Harvey (see Bibliography), pp. 18f. R. de Vaux, "Method in the Study of Early Hebrew History," in *The Bible in Modern Scholarship*, pp. 15-17; "Peut-on écrire une 'théologie de l'AT'?" *Bible et Orient* (Paris, 1967), pp. 59-71.

15 "Israelitisch-jüdische Religionsgeschichte und alttestamentliche Theologie," *ZAW*, 44 (1926), 1-12; cf. the critical response by W. Eichrodt, *infra*, n. 27.

be in competition with systematic theology as the latter expresses itself in the form of system building based on its own categories either with or without the aid of philosophy. Systematic theology will also need to continue its reflection on the application of theology and preaching to the multiplex contemporary issues confronting every Christian. Systematic theology will always have its place in Christian thought. But in contrast to systematic theology, must not the discipline of Biblical theology draw its very principles of presentation from the Bible rather than ecclesiastical documents or scholastic and modern philosophy? Would it not be one of the tasks of Biblical theology to come to grips with the nature of the Biblical texts as aiming beyond themselves, as ontological and theological in their intention and function through the ages, without defining in advance the nature of Biblical reality?

B. *The Confessional Method.* It seems only natural that it has been argued that the confessional method is the only viable option toward a solution of the problem of methodology. This approach is diametrically opposed to the historical descriptive method, which to many only produces a history of the religion of Israel[16] and not an OT theology.[17] The confessional method is based largely upon Eissfeldt's sharp methodological distinction between *Religionsgeschichte*, which is said to be a com-

[16] Th. C. Vriezen, *The Religion of Ancient Israel* (Philadelphia, 1967), p. 7: "My purpose in what follows is to offer a picture of the religion of Israel with respect not only to its *historical* development but to its essence and inmost character as well" (italics mine). According to G. Fohrer, *Geschichte der israelitischen Religion* (Berlin, 1969), pp. 7f., it is the "Aufgabe einer Darstellung der Geschichte der israelitischen Religion den Werdegang dieser Religion als die normale Geschichte einer normalen Religion neben anderen zu schildern, ohne theologische Wertungen vorzunehmen oder apologetische Gesichtspunkte geltend zu machen."

[17] Jacob, *Theology of the OT,* p. 24.

pletely "neutral" discipline[18] in which believer and un-
believer can work together in harmony, and OT theology, which must be done from the standpoint of
faith.[19] Th. C. Vriezen follows Eissfeldt's distinction. The
former's OT theology is a typical example for the confessional method. Vriezen states that OT theology is a
"Christian theological science" which works with "theological standards" and rests "on the ground of its Christian theological starting point."[20] G. A. F. Knight con-
curs.[21] His book may be considered a more extreme

18 The term "neutral criticism" is used by Childs, *Interpretation,* 17
(1964), 432ff., for the purely descriptive approach to the Bible by the
historical-critical method. This type of interpretation he claims defines
in advance the investigator's stance toward Scripture as that of one who
is neutral toward its ultimate claims as revelation. G. E. Wright (in
Translating and Understanding the OT, pp. 298ff.) has criticized the
application of "neutral criticism" as a valid description of the historical-
critical method on the ground that no scholar is really "neutral" in his
descriptive work. Wright has certainly made a valid point. But the
historical-critical method claims to begin from the outset by excluding
the revelatory-divine aspect. If Childs means by his emphasis that exegesis can only begin and remain within a "framework of faith" (which
is defined for the Christian by Jesus Christ), then one would have to
concede that the historical-critical method does not encompass any
religious or "framework of faith" stance (cf. G. Ebeling, "The Significance of the Critical Historical Method for Church and Theology in
Protestantism," in *Word and Faith* [Philadelphia, 1963], pp. 17-61, esp.
47, 50). If this is the case, then it would seem that the method used for
the purely descriptive task is too limited for complete theological
understanding. It may be added parenthetically that G. von Rad, in the
5th German ed. of his *Theologie des AT* (München, 1966), I (hereafter
cited as *TAT*), speaks of a "scheinbar exakt arbeitenden Geschichts-
wissenschaft," which is limited, however, by working without a God-
hypothesis.

19 Eissfeldt, *ZAW,* 44 (1926), 2ff.

20 *An Outline of OT Theology*[2], pp. 147f. It should be noted, however, that in the presentation of his material Vriezen is closer to
Eichrodt.

21 *A Christian Theology of the OT* (2nd ed.; London, 1964), p. 7:
"A Theology of the Old Testament is written with the express presupposition . . . that the Old Testament is nothing less than the Christian
Scripture." Jacob, *Grundfragen alttestamentlicher Theologie,* p. 14,
criticizes Knight for his dubious parallelism Israel = Son of God —
Jesus = Son of God and his unconvincing attempt to prove the unity of
both Testaments.

example of the usage of this method. R. de Vaux, too, follows the emphasis of the confessional method by maintaining that "theology is the science of faith. . . . As a Christian theologian I receive the Old Testament as the Word of God, the word of *my* God."[22]

But the confessional method is hampered also by decisive shortcomings. Are not the supporters of the confessional method under the domination of an outmoded dichotomy? Eissfeldt believes that the problem of theology in the contemporary situation is the tension between absolute and relative, transcendence and immanence, adding that for Biblical science this general problem has narrowed itself down to that of the tension between history and revelation, knowledge and faith. It is likely a consequence of Eissfeldt's Lutheran background that he characterizes the faculty of knowledge as activity, that of faith as passivity. He holds that it is to the benefit of both knowledge and faith that they should be kept strictly apart. Both faculties are legitimate and necessary but there must be no mixture of the two. Applied to the field of religion, this separation of knowledge and faith means that on the basis of the knowledge category the religion of the OT should be treated historically, in the form of *Religionsgeschichte* as a completely neutral and objective discipline in which members of different Christian faiths and even members of other religions can work together in harmony; whereas on the basis of the category of faith the religion of the OT is to be treated as the true religion, as God's revelation, as OT theology, which is a purely confessional matter. The discussion that followed Eissfeldt's proposals has shown that his methodological distinctions, which are on the whole basic for those who carry on the confessional method, are on the one hand dominated by a superseded historical positivism[23] and on the other

22 *Bible et Orient,* p. 66.
23 See Kraus, *Die Biblische Theologie,* p. 311.

by an artificial and unsupportable separation of knowledge and faith.[24] The theologian needs to be warned not
to ground his theological structure upon foundations
which become obsolete with the change of philosophical
premises.[25] The questions that remain unresolved concern whether an OT theology written from "the framework of faith" should be written from the framework of
my faith (Eissfeldt, de Vaux), the Christian faith, or
New Testament faith. Furthermore, we must ask, what
claim to objectivity does such a confessional theology of
the OT have? Would not a theologian of Lutheran background write an OT theology valid only for Lutherans
and one of Catholic background for Catholics, etc.? It
appears that an OT theology needs to maintain its
independence over against confessional or creedal
domination.

C. *The Cross-Section Method.* The foremost repre-
sentative of the cross-section method is W. Eichrodt,
whose monumental work is one of the major contributions to the subject of OT theology in this century.[26] It
is to his credit that he called, as early as 1929, to a
radical reorientation[27] in order to move beyond the im-
passe into which the application of a historico-genetic
principle had led the development of OT theology, from
Georg L. Bauer (1755-1806) to Emil Kautzsch (1911),
under the influence of historicism.[28]

24 Eissfeldt explains that the tension between "knowledge and faith"
needs to be seen in connection with the tension of the absolute and the
relative and the tension between transcendence and immanence which
he considers to be *the* problem of theology.

25 H. J. Iwand, "Um den rechten Glauben," *Gesammelte Aufsätze*
(Göttingen, 1959), p. 174; cf. Kraus, pp. 313f.

26 W. Eichrodt, *Theology of the OT,* trans. J. A. Baker (2 vols.;
Philadelphia, 1961, 1965). Hereafter cited as *TOT,* I and II.

27 W. Eichrodt, "Hat die alttestamentliche Theologie noch selb-
ständige Bedeutung in der alttestamentlichen Wissenschaft?" *ZAW,* 47
(1929), 83-91. Note on the development of the debate Porteous, *The OT
and Modern Study,* pp. 322ff.; and E. G. Kraeling, *The OT Since the
Reformation* (New York, 1969), pp. 270ff.

28 Cf. Dentan, *Preface,* pp. 26-57; Kraus, *Die Biblische Theologie,*
pp. 88-125.

Eichrodt insists correctly that in every science there is a subjective element. Historians have come to take seriously that there is inevitably a subjective element in all historical research worthy of the name. The positivist errs when for the sake of objectivity he attempts to remove all philosophy from the individual sciences. One cannot be a true historian if one ignores the philosophy of history. The historian will always be guided in his work by a principle of selection which is certainly a subjective enterprise and by a goal which gives perspective to his work which is equally subjective. Eichrodt admits that history is unable to make an ultimate pronouncement on the truth or falsity of anything, on its validity or invalidity. He claims that while the OT theologian makes an existential judgment which, in part at least, determines the subjective element to be found in his account of OT religion, there is no countenance to the charge that OT theology is unscientific in character.

Eichrodt's theology remains with both feet planted in history. He maintains that the OT theologian has to be guided by a principle of selection and a principle of congeniality. The great systematic task consists of making a cross-section through the historical process, laying bare the inner structure of religion. His aim is "to understand the realm of OT belief in its structural unity . . . [and] to illuminate its profoundest meaning."[29] Under the conviction that the "tyranny of historicism"[30] must be broken, he explains that "the irruption of the Kingship of God into this world and its establishment here" is "that which binds together indivisibly the two realms of the Old and New Testaments." But in addition to this historical movement from the OT to the New "there is a current of life flowing in reverse direction from the New Testament to the Old."[31] The principle of selection

[29] *TOT*, I, 31.
[30] *Ibid*.
[31] I, 26.

in Eichrodt's theology turns out to be the covenant concept, and the goal that provides perspective is found in the NT.

It is to Eichrodt's credit that he broke once and for all with the traditional God-Man-Salvation arrangement, taken over time and again by Biblical theologians from dogmatics.[32] His procedure for treating the realm of OT thought attempts to have "the historical principle operating side by side with the systematic in a complementary role."[33] The systematic principle Eichrodt finds in the covenant concept, which becomes the overriding and unifying category in his OT theology.[34] Out of the combination of the historical principle and the covenant principle grow Eichrodt's three major categories representing the basic structure of his *magnum opus*, viz. God and the people, God and the world, and God and man.[35] His systematic cross-section treatment is so executed as to exhibit the development of thought and institution within his system. The cross-section method, with Eichrodt's use of the covenant concept as the means whereby unity is achieved, is to some extent artificial, since the OT is less amenable to systematization than Eichrodt suggests.

Eichrodt's cross-section method has its serious problems. Within his presentation one finds explications of

[32] The OT theologies of E. König (Stuttgart, 1923), E. Sellin (Leipzig, 1933), and L. Köhler (Tübingen, 1935) were still to a larger or smaller degree dependent on the Theology-Anthropology-Soteriology arrangement of systematic theology which became dominant in the post-Gabler period in Biblical theology.

[33] Eichrodt, *TOT*, I, 17ff.

[34] I, 32.

[35] H. Schultz, *Alttestamentliche Theologie. Die Offenbarungsreligion in ihrer vorchristlichen Entwicklungsstufe* (5th ed.; Leipzig, 1896), had already anticipated Eichrodt in the systematic arrangement of the second part of his OT theology. Eichrodt, *TOT*, I, 33 n. 1, confesses that he owes his three major categories to the outline by Otto Procksch, *Theologie des AT* (Gütersloh, 1950), pp. 420-713.

"historical developments"[36] in which the religio-historical view comes through but hardly ever the prospect to the NT! This is especially surprising since he claims there is a "two-way relationship between the Old and New Testament," and contends that without this relationship "we do not find a correct definition of the problem of OT theology."[37] In this respect his work is hardly an improvement over the earlier history-of-religions approaches. Furthermore, the systematic principle, i.e., the covenant concept, with which Eichrodt operates attempts to enclose within its grasp the diversified thoughts of the OT. It is here that the problem of the cross-section method lies. Is the covenant concept, or Vriezen's community concept, or any other single concept, sufficiently comprehensive to include within it all variety of OT thoughts?[38] In more general terms, is the OT a world of thought or belief that can be systematized in such a way?[39] Does one not lose the comprehensive perspective of history with the compartmentalization of

[36] For example, the history of the covenant concept and the history of the prophetic movement in *TOT*, I, 36ff., 309ff. The phrase "historical development" is used by Eichrodt himself, I, 32.

[37] I, 26.

[38] Inasmuch as Wright, *The OT and Theology*, p. 62, has recently given support to the centrality of the covenant concept for the recitation of the acts of God and thus to Eichrodt's methodology, one needs to call to mind also his earlier strictures with regard to the adequacy of the covenant concept. Wright stated in *Studia Biblica et Semitica*, p. 377: "It is improbable, however, that any one single theme is sufficiently comprehensive to include within it all variety." Cf. the critique of the cipher/symbol of covenant by Norman R. Gottwald, "W. Eichrodt, Theology of the OT," in *Contemporary OT Theologians*, pp. 53-56.

[39] Wright, *Studia Biblica et Semitica*, p. 383, makes the point that "the event-centered mode of God's revelation cannot be systematized, for it includes both the confessional recital of God's activity and the inferences and deductions which a worshipping community draws from it in the variety of historical situations in which it finds itself." W. Richter, "Beobachtungen zur theologischen Systembildung in der alttestamentlichen Literatur anhand des 'kleinen geschichtlichen Credo'," in *Wahrheit und Verkündigung. M. Schmaus zum 70. Geburtstag* (München, 1967), p. 175, states categorically that "no theology of the Old Testament can do without a comprehensive principle according to which the presentation of the material must group itself."

single thematic perspectives under one single common denominator? Is it not a basic inadequacy of the cross-section method as a tool of inquiry that it remains schizophrenically stretched in the tension of historical summary and theological pointer?

It seems inevitable that the Biblical theologian must in the last analysis become somewhat systematic. While it is to be admitted that he inevitably modifies the meaning of the Biblical terms, motifs, and concepts by his personal reflection and exposition, his endeavor must therefore be radically controlled in order that he does not succumb to the temptation of reducing the word of God to what he can handle by means of *his* clear and distinct ideas, which may be in no wise close to or identical with that of the Biblical testimony. Is it not impossible to do justice to the multiform and multiplex nature of the Biblical witness in attempting to grasp the richness of the Biblical testimonies by a unilinear approach determined by one single concept, whether it be covenant, election, kingdom of God, rulership of God, communion, or something else? The richness of the diversified nature of the Biblical testimony requires an approach that is commensurate to the materials with which it deals.

D. *The Diachronic Method.* A new methodological approach for OT theology, one that deserves to be put in a class by itself, is that of Gerhard von Rad.[40] For

---

[40] G. von Rad, *OT Theology* (2 vols.; New York, 1962, 1966), hereafter cited as *OTT*, I and II. Many important reviews are cited by G. Henton Davies, "Gerhard von Rad, OT Theology," in *Contemporary OT Theologians*, pp. 65-89. The following articles deal largely with the problems raised by von Rad: F. Hesse, "Die Erforschung der Geschichte als theologische Aufgabe," *Kerygma und Dogma*, 4 (1958), 1-19; "Kerygma oder geschichtliche Wirklichkeit?" *ZThK*, 57 (1960), 17-26; "Bewährt sich eine 'Theologie der Heilstatsachen' am AT? Zum Verhältnis von Faktum und Deutung?" *ZThK*, 81 (1969), 1-17; V. Maag, "Historische und ausserhistorische Begründung alttestamentlicher Theologie," *Schweizer Theologische Umschau*, 29 (1959), 6-18; F. Baumgärtel, "Gerhard von Rads Theologie des AT," *ThLZ*, 86 (1961), 801-816, 895-

lack of a better term we may call his the diachronic method.[41] His OT theology needs to be understood as the theology of the historical and prophetic traditions. Though he prefaces his theology of the traditions with a sketch of the history of Yahwism and Israelite sacral institutions as reconstructed by the historical - critical method, he states that "historical investigation searches for a critically assured minimum — the kerygmatic picture tends toward a theological maximum." This means for von Rad that an OT theology cannot do justice to the content of the OT through a presentation of the minimum. The OT theologian must recognize that the "kerygmatic picture" as painted by the faith of Israel is also "founded in the actual history and is not invented."[42] As a matter of fact "Israel with her testimonies speaks from such a deep level of historical experience which historical-critical research is unable to reach."[43] Thus the subject of an OT theology is above all "this world made up of testimonies" and not "a systematic ordered world of faith" or thought.[44] This world of "testimonies," that is, "what Israel herself testified concerning Jahweh,"[45] namely "the word and deed of Jahweh in history,"[46] presents neither pure revelation

908; Ch. Barth, "Grundprobleme einer Theologie des AT," *EvTh*, 23 (1963), 342-372; M. Honecker, "Zum Verständnis der Geschichte in Gerhard von Rads Theologie des AT," *EvTh*, 23 (1963), 143-168; H. Graf Reventlow, "Grundfragen einer alttestamentlichen Theologie im Lichte der neueren deutschen Forschung," *ThZ*, 17 (1961), 81ff.; Gerhard F. Hasel, "The Problem of History in OT Theology," *AUSS*, 8 (1970), 23-50; Harvey, *Biblical Theology Bulletin*, 1 (1971), 9ff.

[41] This term is used by Harvey, p. 5, whereby we may understand the description of *longitudinal* sections of the OT with special attention to the *chronological* sequence of the various traditions and books in contrast to the cross-section method with the thematic arrangement.

[42] *TAT*, I, 120; *OTT*, I, 108.

[43] *TAT*, I, 120. *OTT*, I, does not have this sentence since it was translated from the 2nd German edition.

[44] *TAT*, I, 124; *OTT*, I, 111. Von Rad here goes contrary to the approach of Eichrodt.

[45] *TAT*, I, 118; *OTT*, I, 105.

[46] *TAT*, I, 127; *OTT*, I, 114.

from above nor pure perception and presentation from below but is "drawn up by faith" and is accordingly "confessional in character."[47] It is these confessional statements of the "continuing activity of God in history"[48] that are the proper subject-matter of an OT theology. It is obvious that with von Rad kerygma theology has broken with all might into the field of OT studies.[49]

Von Rad emphasizes the more complete "kerygmatic picture" with the deeper dimensions of reality as the one which OT theology must explicate. But is not this kind of theologizing, which is based upon the confessional and thus kerygmatic testimonies of the OT, still very unrelated to the historical-critical reconstruction of Israel's history, inasmuch as the latter does not coincide with the kerygmatic picture of OT faith and history? This is precisely the point von Rad likes to make. For him the historian's reconstructed picture of Israel's history is impoverished and therefore unable to be the basis for explicating the total reality contained in the OT testimonies, with which an OT theology must concern itself. Because of this he focuses on the OT interpretation in his theology, rather than basing his OT theology on the historical-critical interpretation of events whose historicity is not in question. Whereas this is a step in the right direction, the history von Rad envisages too often itself falls short of the OT testimonies, because it is merely history of tradition, or historical experiences influencing traditions. To this crucial point in his theological endeavor we need to return, because it raises the problem of the relation of *Traditionsgeschichte* to *Historie* and *Heilsgeschichte*.

The matter of presenting OT theology is defined by

[47] *TAT*, I, 119; *OTT*, I, 107.
[48] *TAT*, I, 118; *OTT*, I, 106.
[49] Eichrodt, *TOT*, I, 515. See here also the interpretation of von Rad by O. Cullmann, *Salvation in History* (New York, 1967), pp. 54ff. On Cullmann's understanding and usage of von Rad, see Kraus, *Die Biblische Theologie*, pp. 186ff.

von Rad in a new way. "Re-telling [*Nacherzählen*] remains the most legitimate form of theological discourse
on the Old Testament."[50] What does von Rad understand
by "re-telling"? How is the theologian or preacher to
proceed? Is he just to relate, i.e., to tell again, what the
OT has told without translating it theologically for
modern man?

It appears that von Rad has chosen the notion of
"re-telling" because he refuses to construe a new system.
In his view any system is alien to the nature of the OT.
In this we might easily agree with him. Von Rad is also
unable to find a "center [*Mitte*]"[51] in the OT. For these
reasons he limits himself to narrating what the OT says
about its own contents. He emphasizes that since Israel
stated her kerygmatic-confessional testimonies in historical statements, we cannot state it in any other way
except in a rehearsal of the narrative. The problem that
this method produces for applied theology is immense.

With regard to this problem F. Baumgärtel asks how
one can speak, for example, in a theologically legitimate
way about Hosea 1 — 3 when one merely retells what is
stated there? How does this retelling proceed? In what
way is it, whenever it takes place, the legitimate theological discourse on the OT?[52] One may surmise that
the criticism concerning the ambiguous notion of re-
telling caused von Rad to place less emphasis on it in
more recent years.[53]

E. *The NT Quotation Method.* The most recent

[50] *TAT*, I, 135; *OTT*, I, 121, "Re-telling" as the most appropriate
form of presenting the OT has been supported by Ch. Barth, *EvTh*, 23
(1963), 346; H.-J. Stoebe, "Überlegungen zur Theologie des AT," *Gottes
Wort und Gottes Land. H.-W. Hertzberg zum 70. Geburtstag,* ed. H.
Graf Reventlow (Göttingen, 1965), p. 206; F. Mildenberger, *Die halbe
Wahrheit oder die ganze Schrift* (München, 1967), pp. 79ff.

[51] *TAT*, II, 376; *OTT*, II, 362; cf. Hasel, *AUSS*, 8 (1970), 25-29.

[52] *ThLZ*, 86 (1961), 903f.

[53] In von Rad's important article "Offene Fragen im Umkreis einer
Theologie des AT," *ThLZ*, 88 (1963), 401-416, the notion of *Nacherzählen* recedes completely.

clearly outlined methodological approach to OT theology comes from B. S. Childs.[54] He proposes "a form of Biblical Theology that takes as its primary task the disciplined theological reflection of the Bible in the context of the canon."[55] This means in particular that the categories for OT theology must "begin with specific Old Testament passages which are quoted within the New Testament."[56] On the basis of this unique starting-point we may be justified in calling the method as developed by Childs the NT quotation method.

The NT quotation method grows out of the concern to take seriously the Scriptural canon as the context for Biblical theology.[57] "To do Biblical Theology within the context of the canon involves acknowledgment of the *normative* quality of the Biblical tradition."[58] This emphasis on the part of Childs must be considered as his attempt to overcome a major weak point of the American Biblical Theology Movement, namely "its failure to take the Biblical text seriously in its canonical form." The Biblical Theology Movement came to the text from a vantage point "outside the text,"[59] namely liberal historical criticism with its liberal hermeneutic presupposition. For Childs "the confession of a canon opposes . . . attempts at separating the text from reality." This impossible tension in the Biblical Theology Movement was caused by the strain of using orthodox Biblical language for the constructive part of theology, but at the same time approaching the Bible with all the assumptions of liberalism. In this connection Childs notes that "one of the major factors in the breakdown of the Bib-

[54] The shape of Childs' new Biblical theology has found its most complete expression to date in his *Biblical Theology in Crisis*, pp. 91-122.

[55] P. 122.

[56] Pp. 114f.

[57] Pp. 99-106.

[58] P. 100 (italics his).

[59] P. 102.

lical Theology Movement was its total failure to come to grips with the inspiration of Scripture."[60] Childs hopes to avoid the same mistake in his approach by taking seriously the canon as the context for Biblical theology in that the canon as context "offers another alternative in respect to the inspiration of Scripture."[61]

Does the NT quotation method prove to be a more adequate method? One of the problems of this method concerns the matter of the relationship between the Testaments. The subtle move from the NT to the OT is not at all obvious. Childs presupposes an *analogia fidei* between the Testaments. While he admits that a NT quotation of an OT passage might not necessarily be identical in its witness but may complement the other or stand indeed in sharp tension,[62] there remains nevertheless the problematical move in a single direction, namely from the NT to the OT. One wonders whether there is not a natural and fully justified move from the OT to the NT. The NT quotation method has in actuality hardly any room at all for the move from the OT to the NT, because the unique starting-point is the NT. Is there any sound historical and theological basis for such a one-way move? Though Childs wants to stay within the Scriptural canon, he actually does employ an external key for unlocking the OT. Any possible reciprocal relationship between the Testaments is thwarted from the outset by this limited NT starting-point.

Another serious objection to be advanced against this method is that the NT's use of the OT is limited.[63] Where for example has the rich wisdom theology of the OT room in such an approach? The OT wisdom theology would be relegated as in von Rad's approach to the status of a stepchild. Despite the variety of the NT's use

60 P. 103.

61 P. 104.

62 P. 112.

63 Childs is aware of this problem but is not able to solve it; pp. 115f.

of the OT, the OT testimony has a richness, diversity, and variety that is not encompassed in the NT. In view of Childs' admission that there are to be moves from the OT to the NT as well as the reverse in a presentation of OT theology,[64] he is not faithful to his own methodological discussion when he limits the approach for doing OT theology to deal only with OT quotations in the NT. Here the movement becomes decidedly a limited one-way road.[65] Such limitations render the NT quotation method incapable of coming to grips with the full richness and depth of the Biblical testimony.

[64] Pp. 113, 114.

[65] The Biblical theologian engaged in doing NT theology may ask what kind of method he is to follow. Is he to derive his rubrics for doing NT theology from NT quotations in the Didache or other early Christian documents or is he to revert to the Apostolic Fathers or later material? It seems certain that a method for doing Biblical theology needs to be such that it may serve in broad perspectives for both Testaments. If this is not the case, then one would never be able to come to a truly Biblical theology that encompasses both Testaments.

II. The Question of History, History of Tradition, and Salvation History

A cluster of questions connected with the proper understanding of history has come to the center of attention due especially to von Rad's theology.[1] He poses the problem in its acutest form through his sharp antithetical contrast of the two versions of Israel's history, namely that of "modern critical research and that which Israel's faith has built up."[2] We have already seen that the picture of Israel's history as reconstructed with the historical-critical method, in von Rad's terms, "searches for a critically assured minimum — the kerygmatic picture [of Israel's history as built up by its faith] tends toward a theological maximum."[3] Von Rad feels that the dichotomy of the two pictures of Israel's history is a "difficult historical problem."[4] But he emphatically asserts that the subject of a theology of the OT must deal with the "world made up of testimonies"[5] as built up by Israel's faith, i.e., with the kerygmatic picture of Israel's history, because in the OT "there are no *bruta facta* at all; we have history only in the form of in-

[1] See Hasel, *AUSS*, 8 (1970), 29-32, 36-46.
[2] This phrase is found in the 1st ed. of *TAT*, I, 8, a section unfortunately not translated in *OTT*.
[3] *TAT*, I, 120; *OTT*, I, 108.
[4] *TAT*, I, 119; *OTT*, I, 106.
[5] *TAT*, I, 124; *OTT*, I, 111.

terpretation, only in reflection."[6] It is crucial to von Rad's argumentation that in the historical-critical picture of Israel's history no premises of faith or revelation are taken into account since the historical-critical method works without a God-hypothesis.[7] Israel, however, "could only understand her history as a road along which she travelled under Yahweh's guidance. For Israel, history existed only where Yahweh has revealed himself through acts and word."[8] Von Rad rejects the either-or choice of considering the kerygmatic picture as unhistorical and the historical-critical picture as historical. He contends that "the kerygmatic picture too . . . is founded in actual history and has not been invented." Nevertheless, he speaks of the "early historical experiences" of primeval history in terms of "historical poetry," "legend [Sage]," "poetic stories"[9] containing "anachronisms."[10] The important thing for von Rad is not "that the historical kernel is overlaid with fiction" but that the experience of the horizon of the later narrator's own faith as read into the saga is "historical"[11] and results in a great enrichment of the saga's theological content. For von Rad the emphasis of the history of tradition method is again dominant.

Although the problem of the dichotomous pictures of Israel's history is not new,[12] von Rad's position has pro-

[6] This is the point made by von Rad, "Antwort auf Conzelmanns Fragen," *EvTh*, 24 (1964), 393, in his dispute with the NT scholar Hans Conzelmann, "Fragen an Gerhard von Rad," *EvTh*, 24 (1964), 113-125.

[7] *ThLZ*, 88 (1963), 408ff.; *OTT*, II, 417.

[8] *ThLZ*, 88 (1963), 409. The translation of these sentences in *OTT*, II, 418, does not reflect accurately the original emphasis. The problem of the relationship of word and event, word and acts, etc., is a subject of special discussion in Hasel, *AUSS*, 8 (1970), 32-36.

[9] *TAT*, I, 120-122; *OTT*, I, 108f.

[10] *OTT*, II, 421f.; *ThLZ*, 88 (1963), 411f.

[11] *OTT*, II, 421.

[12] Toward the end of the 19th century, scholarship in general corrected the Biblical picture when it was felt that it was in conflict with historical knowledge without recognizing that it may contain a considerable theological problem. (Cf. C. Westermann, "Zur Auslegung des

duced a lively and even spirited debate. Von Rad assumed that the two diverging pictures of Israel's history could "for the present"[13] simply stand next to each other with OT theology expounding the kerygmatic one and largely ignoring the historical-critical one. Franz Hesse, taking up von Rad's thesis that the OT "is a history book [*Geschichtsbuch*],"[14] promptly turns this thesis against him by arguing that unique theological relevance must be given to Israel's history as reconstructed by the historical-critical method.[15] This alone is theologically relevant.[16] Our faith needs to rest upon "that which has actually happened and not that which is confessed to have happened but about which we have to admit that it did not happen in that way."[17] Hesse turns against what he calls von Rad's "double tracking," namely, that the secular history is to deal with the history of Israel while the kerygmatic version is theologically meaningful.[18] He marks out the difference

---

AT," *Vergegenwärtigung. Aufsätze zur Auslegung des AT* [Berlin, 1955], p. 100.) Opponents to Wellhausenism recognized the deep rift. A. Köhler, *Lehrbuch der Biblischen Geschichte Alten Testaments* (Erlangen, 1875), I, iv, distinguished between a secular and theological discipline of Biblical history, claiming that it is the theologian's task "to study and to retell the course of OT history as the authors of the OT understood it." Both pictures have to stand independently next to each other. J. Köberle, "Heilsgeschichtliche und religionsgeschichtliche Betrachtungsweise des AT," *Neue Kirchliche Zeitschrift,* 17 (1906), 200-222, to the contrary, wants to give theological validity only to the real history of Israel as reached by modern methodology. J. Hempel, "AT und Geschichte," in *Studien des apologetischen Seminars,* 27 (Gütersloh, 1930), pp. 80-83, believes that an objectively erroneous report about the past may not oppose the reality of divine revelation. It still remains *that* God has acted even if it is in question *how* he did it. G. E. Wright, *God Who Acts,* p. 115, makes the distinction between history and recital of history by faith where discrepancies, however, are only a "minor feature" (p. 126). Theology must deal with and communicate life, reason, and faith which are part of one whole.

13 *TAT,* I, 119; *OTT,* I, 107.
14 *TAT,* II, 370; *OTT,* II, 415.
15 *ZThK,* 57 (1960), 24f.; *ZAW,* 89 (1969), 3.
16 *ZAW,* 89 (1969), 6.
17 *ZThK,* 57 (1960), 26.
18 *Kerygma und Dogma,* IV (1958), 5-8.

between the two pictures of Israel's history with des-
ignations such as "real" and "unreal" or "correct" and
"incorrect." He maintains that the version of Israel's
history as drawn up by historical - critical research is
alone theologically relevant, because judged against the
results of historical-critical research the picture which
Israel herself has drawn up is not only open to error but
in very fact contains too often error. An OT theology
must consist of "more than pure description of Old
Testament tradition. . . . Our faith lives from that which
happened in Old Testament times, not from that which
is confessed as having happened. . . . Kerygma is not
constitutive for our faith, but historical reality is."[19]
Thus Hesse attempts to overcome the dichotomy of the
two versions of Israel's history by closely identifying
the historical - critical picture of Israel's history with
salvation history.[20] He states: "In what the people of
Israel in the centuries of its existence experienced, what
it did and what it suffered, 'salvation history' is present.
This [salvation history] does not run side by side with
the history of Israel, it does not lie upon another 'higher'
plane, but although it is not identical with the history
of Israel it is nevertheless there; thus we can say that
in, with, and beneath the history of Israel God leads his
salvation history to the 'telos' Jesus Christ, that is to
say, in, with, and beneath that which happens, which
actually took place."[21] Hesse therefore contends that "a
separation between the history of Israel and Old Testament salvation history is thus not possible," for "salvation history is present in hidden form in, with, and beneath the history of Israel."[22] From this it follows that
the totality of "the history of the people of Israel with
all its features is the subject of theological research. . . ."[23]

[19] *ZThK*, 57 (1960), 24f.
[20] See also Honecker, pp. 158f.
[21] *Kerygma und Dogma*, IV, 10 (italics his).
[22] P. 13.
[23] P. 19.

Hesse grounds saving history solely in the historical-critical version of Israel's history, insisting upon the "facticity of that which is reported," so that "the witness of Israel about its own history is not to concern us in as far as it wants to be witness of history, because it stands and falls with the historicity of that which is witnessed."[24] This seems to indicate that the kerygma of the OT as well as the kerygmatic version of Israel's history is to be judged by the historicity of that which is witnessed by it.[25]

It is to be conceded that the historical-critical picture of Israel's history plays a historic role in modern times. But Hesse's one-sided emphasis is due to his unique confidence in modern historiography. He actually falls prey to historical positivism. He apparently does not recognize that the historical-critical version of Israel's history is also already interpreted history, namely, interpreted on the basis of historico-philosophical premises. Both von Rad[26] and F. Mildenberger[27] emphasize this point. Another serious stricture against Hesse's thesis concerns his seeking to attribute to the historical-critical picture of Israel's history a historic role in NT times. "God's history with Israel leading to the goal Jesus Christ is to be traced where history really happened. . . ."[28] But OT history as it is perceived today with the historical-critical method was unknown in NT times. On this point James M. Robinson adds that "to relate only this historical-critical history with the goal

24 *ZThK*, 57 (1960), 25f.

25 *Kerygma und Dogma*, IV, 17-19.

26 Von Rad points out that the version of Israel's history given by modern historiography is already interpreted history; *TAT*, II, 9: "Auch das Bild der modernen Historie ist gedeutete Geschichte und zwar von geschichtsphilosophischen Prämissen aus, die für das Handeln Gottes in der Geschichte keinerlei Wahrnehmungsmöglichkeiten ergeben, weil hier notorisch nur der Mensch als der Schöpfer seiner Geschichte verstanden wird."

27 *Gottes Tat im Wort* (Gütersloh, 1964), p. 31 n. 37.

28 *Kerygma und Dogma*, IV, 11.

in Jesus Christ is to conceive of that history in an un-
historic way."[29] J. A. Soggin designates Hesse's attempt
as an easy retreat behind modern historiography insofar
as he seeks to get rid of the risk which the incarnate
Word of God has taken upon itself.[30] Eva Osswald
points out that Hesse seeks a purely historical solution
to the problem and that therefore history as the scene
of God's action recedes into the background.[31] In my
opinion it is methodologically not possible to abstract
an actual event or fact from the confessional-kerygmatic
tradition of Israel with the historical-critical method,
and then to designate this "factual happening" as the
action of God, thereby making it theologically
relevant.[32]

In connection with Hesse's approach it is significant
that the historical-critical picture of Israel's history is
by no means a unified picture. We should remind ourselves that the historical-critical method has produced
two versions of the proto-history, viz. the version of the
school of Alt-Noth on the one hand and that of the
school of Albright-Wright-Bright[33] on the other, not to

[29] "The Historicality of Biblical Language," *The OT and Christian
Faith*, ed. B. W. Anderson (New York, 1963), p. 126.

[30] "Alttestamentliche Glaubenszeugnisse und geschichtliche Wirklichkeit," *ThZ*, 17 (1960), 388; "Geschichte, Historie und Heilsgeschichte,"
ThLZ, 89 (1964), 721ff.

[31] "Geschehene und geglaubte Geschichte," *Wissenschaftliche Zeitschrift der Universität Jena*, 14 (1965), 707.

[32] See here Mildenberger's incisive criticism of Hesse, in *Gottes Tat
im Wort*, p. 42 n. 67. In view of these observations it is difficult to conceive how J. M. Robinson, "Heilsgeschichte und Lichtungsgeschichte,"
EvTh, 22 (1962), 118, can speak of a "basic strength of Hesse's position"
over against that of von Rad.

[33] See especially M. Weippert, *Die Landnahme der israelitischen
Stämme in der neueren wissenschaftlichen Diskussion* (*FRLANT*, 92;
Göttingen, 1967), pp. 14-140; R. de Vaux, *Die Patriarchenerzählungen
und ihre Religion* (2nd ed.; Stuttgart, 1968), pp. 126-167; and R. de
Vaux, "Method in the Study of Early Hebrew History," *The Bible in
Modern Scholarship*, pp. 15-29; and the response by G. E. Mendenhall,
pp. 30-36.

speak of the views of Mendenhall.[34] In addition there are a host of unsolved problems in the later period according to these historical-critical pictures of Israel's history, so that it is an illusion to speak of *a* or *the* scientific picture of Israel's history, for such a picture is just not available.[35] Thus the attempt to ground theology solely on the so-called historical-critical picture of Israel's history falls short on account of decisive and insurmountable shortcomings.

Walther Eichrodt also objects vehemently to von Rad's establishing such a dualism between the two pictures of Israel's history. He feels that the rift between the two pictures of Israel's history "is wrenched apart with such violence . . . that it seems impossible henceforth to restore an inner coherence between the aspects of Israel's history." Von Rad dissolved the "true history of Israel" into "religious poetry"; even worse, it is drawn up by Israel "in flat contradiction of the facts."[36] It seems that Eichrodt's negative reaction is centered in his distinction of the "external facts" of saving history in the OT from the "decisive inward event," namely, "the interior overmastering of the human spirit by God's personal invasion."[37] Here, in the creation and development of God's people, in the realization of the covenant relationship, the "decisive" event takes place "without which all external facts must become myth."[38] Here, then, is the "point of origin for all further relation in history, here is the possibility and norm for all state-

[34]"The Hebrew Conquest of Palestine," *Biblical Archaeologist*, 25 (1962), 66-87. Note the critical discussion by one belonging to the Alt-Noth school, Weippert, *Die Landnahme*, pp. 66-69.

[35]Soggin, *ThZ*, 17 (1961), 385-387.

[36]*TOT*, I, 512f.

[37]*TOT*, I, 15.

[38]*TOT*, I, 15f.; also Eichrodt, *Theologie des AT*, II/III (4th ed.; Göttingen, 1961), p. XII. It is to be regretted that much of the important discussion contained in the introductory section of the German edition is omitted in English.

ments about God's speech and deed."[39] In reality, however, the faith of Israel is "founded on facts of history"
and only in this way can this faith have "any kind of
binding authority."[40] Thus it appears that a reconciliation of both versions of Israel's history is in Eichrodt's
thinking not only possible, but in the interest of the
trustworthiness of the biblical witness absolutely
necessary.[41]

Friedrich Baumgärtel sees the weakness of von Rad's
starting-point not so much in the question concerning
the meaning of Israel's confession for Christian faith.
This question cannot be answered by historical research
but must be answered theologically.[42] His criticism is
directed against von Rad's attempt to solve the theological question concerning the meaning of the OT for
Christian faith (phenomenologically) with the aid of
traditio-historical interpretation. For Baumgärtel neither
of the two versions of Israel's history possesses theological relevance for Christian faith. Why? Because
the problem is that the whole OT is "witness out of a
non-Christian religion."[43] "Viewed historically it has
another place than the Christian religion."[44] Thus according to Baumgärtel, von Rad's error lies in assuming
that Israel's witness to God's actions in history can be
taken at face value and as relevant for the Christian

[39] *Theologie des AT*, II/III, p. VIII.
[40] *TOT*, I, 517.
[41] *TOT*, I, 516: " . . . It is realized that in the OT we are dealing
not with an anti-historical transformation of the course of history into
fairy tale or poem, but with an interpretation of real events. . . . Such
interpretation is able, by means of a one-sided rendering, or one exag-
gerated in a particular direction, to grasp and represent the true meaning
of the event more correctly than could an unobjectionable chronicle of
the actual course of history."
[42] "Gerhard von Rads 'Theologie des AT'," *ThLZ*, 86 (1961), 805.
[43] "Das hermeneutische Problem des AT," *ThLZ*, 79 (1954), 200;
"The Hermeneutical Problem of the OT," in *Essays on OT Hermeneutics*, ed. C. Westermann (Richmond, Va., 1963), p. 135. Hereafter cited
as *EOTH*.
[44] *EOTH*, p. 145.

church. The apt reply of another OT theologian, Claus Westermann, is hardly an overstatement: "Ultimately he [Baumgärtel] admits, then, that the church could also live without the Old Testament."[45] The essential weakness of Baumgärtel's criticism of von Rad at this point lies in his ultimate denial of the relevance of the OT for Christian faith.

Another solution to the problem is sought by Johannes Hempel and Eva Osswald. The former maintains that even "an objectively mistaken report about the past, which has part in the lack of trustworthiness of human tradition,"[46] can be a witness about the activity of God, even if it is only a broken witness. According to Hempel it remains established that God has acted in history even if it is an open question how he acted. The investigation of the "how" is according to Hempel also part of the historian's task.[47] Osswald is not able to follow Hempel. She believes that "one cannot always in a clear manner answer how Yahweh has acted with Israel. Thus the only witness that remains is *that* Yahweh has acted with Israel."[48] The distinction between the "thatness" and the "howness,"[49] not unfamiliar from NT studies,[50] can

[45] "Remarks on the Theses of Bultmann and Baumgärtel," *EOTH*, p. 133.

[46] *Studien des apologetischen Seminars*, 27, pp. 80f.

[47] *Geschichten und Geschichte im AT bis zur persischen Zeit* (Gütersloh, 1964), p. 38: "[Der] Historiker [hat] dem Geschichtsstoff des A. T. gegenüber eine doppelte Aufgabe: Er hat nach den Geschehnissen zu Fragen, die den Glauben Israels an das Geschichtswalten seines Gottes geweckt, geformt und im Laufe der Jahrhunderte modifiziert haben, das heisst, er hat zu untersuchen, wieweit der für die Aussagen selbst unveräusserliche Anspruch auf ihre volle Faktizität verifizierbar ist oder nicht. Er hat nach den Glaubensgedanken Israels zu fragen die bei der Ausformung der geschichtlichen Tradition, aber auch bereits bei der Apperzeption des einzelnen Widerfahrnisses wirksam gewesen sind."

[48] Osswald, p. 709.

[49] M. Sekine, "Vom Verstehen der Heilsgeschichte. Das Grundproblem der alttestamentlichen Theologie," *ZAW*, 75 (1963), 145-154, follows Hempel in distinguishing *dicta*, i.e., Biblical statements, from *facta* historical facts. The former are always based upon the latter; both are inseparable in the Bible. Therefore the object of a Biblical theology is *facta dicta*, declared facts which make up salvation history. Up to the

hardly be considered to provide the solution to the problem, because in the final analysis it finds its absolute claim to truth solely in modern historiography. But modern historiography is unable to speak about God's acts.[51] This Osswald concedes. "With the aid of the critical science [of historiography] one is certainly not able to make statements about God, for there is no path that leads from the objectifying science of historiography to a particular theological statement."[52] Thus one is forced to ask whether an event is not grasped in a basically deeper dimension in the given Biblical testimony which sees and presents reality in relationship to a history in which God brings about the salvation of his people.[53]

Here the question has been raised whether or not it is materially pertinent to stress either the historical facts or the confessional kerygma, which is of course also based on facts. A. Weiser and Hempel[54] have recognized that

---

present some have placed either a onesided emphasis upon the *facta* (e.g., Hesse, Eichrodt) or upon the *dicta* (von Rad, Rendtorff). Attempts to bridge the disparity between both have so far been unsuccessful. In the OT existential thought connects *facta* and *dicta* with typology. Thus structural typology is a relevant method. One must ask critically whether this constitutes a superimposing upon the material of something that is alien to the material itself.

[50] Typical of this dilemma is the debate about the "new quest" of the historical Jesus.

[51] A. Weiser, "Vom Verstehen des AT," *ZAW*, 61 (1945/48), 23f., explains that the rational cognition of history is limited to the temporal-spatial dimension, and that the dimension of the knowledge of God can be gained only through the cognition of faith. Cf. Osswald, p. 711: "Faith is not directed upon single historical events, but upon God as the Lord of history."

[52] Osswald, p. 711.

[53] This is the point made by W. Beyerlin, "Geschichte und 'heilsgeschichtliche' Traditionsbildung im AT," *VT*, 13 (1963), 25, with regard to the Gideon tradition and its historical reality.

[54] A. Weiser, *Glaube und Geschichte im AT und andere ausgewählte Schriften* (München, 1961), pp. 2, 22; J. Hempel, "Die Faktizität der Geschichte im biblischen Denken," in *Biblical Studies in Memory of H. C. Alleman* (Locust Valley, N. Y., 1960), pp. 67ff.; *Geschichten und Geschichte*, pp. 11ff. Note also R. H. Pfeiffer, "Facts and Faith in Biblical History," *JBL*, 70 (1951), 1-14; J. C. Rylaarsdam, "The Problem of Faith and History in Biblical Interpretation," *JBL*, 77 (1958), 26-32;

historical reality and kerygmatic expression, i.e., fact and interpretation, form a unity in the OT.[55] Georg Fohrer holds that if there is an essential unity between fact and interpretation, event and word, then we should not pitch one against the other, because the OT authors used traditions that they considered "historical."[56] Hempel shows that the Biblical narrators do not know the tension between report and event which exists for modern man. This had no importance for them at all because they were convinced about the facticity of what had happened.[57] Osswald believes that the facticity of what had happened is binding only for the ancient author, however, and not for modern man, who has raised many doubts by means of modern historiography.[58] We are thrown back upon the question of what measuring rod is applied to establish "facticity." In view of the Biblical testimony the historical-critical method working without a God-hypothesis of which Scripture testifies brings with it a crisis of objectivity and facticity. The question arises whether we do not need to develop, in order to over-

---

C. Blackman, "Is History Irrelevant for the Christian Kerygma?" *Interpretation*, 21 (1967), 435-446; C. E. Braaten, *History and Hermeneutics* (Philadelphia, 1966); "The Current Controversy on Revelation: Pannenberg and His Critics," *Journal of Religion*, 45 (1965), 225-237; J. Barr, "Revelation Through History in the OT and in Modern Theology," *Interpretation*, 17 (1963), 193-205.

[55] W. Pannenberg, "The Revelation of God in Jesus Christ," *Theology as History* (New Frontiers in Theology, III; New York, 1967), p. 127, proposes also that "we must reinstate today the original unity of facts and their meaning." That is to say that "in principle, every event has its original meaning within the context of occurrence and tradition in which it took place. . . ." He says further, "the knowledge of history on which faith is grounded has to do with the truth and reliability of that on which faith depends. . . . Such knowledge . . . assures faith about its basis" (p. 269).

[56] "Tradition und Interpretation im AT," *ZAW*, 73 (1961), 18.

[57] Hempel, *Biblical Studies*, pp. 67ff.; "Faktum und Gesetz im alttestamentlichen Geschichtsdenken," *ThLZ*, 85 (1960), 823ff.; *Geschichten und Geschichte*, pp. 11ff.

[58] Osswald, p. 710.

come the present dilemma, a new set of concepts[59] which is more appropriate to the dynamic nature and full reality of the texts that admittedly encompass the unity of *facta* and *dicta*, fact and interpretation, event and word, happening and meaning.

An attempt of major proportions to come to grips with the problem of the two pictures of Israel's history and salvation history (*Heilsgeschichte*) has been undertaken by Wolfhart Pannenberg, now professor of systematic theology at Munich, who has presented a forceful criticism of current theological positions from the viewpoint, derived from the OT, that "history is the most comprehensive horizon of Christian theology."[60] Pannenberg's

[59] Von Rad, *TAT*, I, 120, focuses our attention on the observation "that Israel's expression derives from a layer of depth of historical experience which historical-critical investigation is unable to fathom."

[60] This sentence opens the essay "Heilsgeschehen und Geschichte," *Kerygma und Dogma*, V (1959), 218-237, 259-288, whose first part is translated as "Redemptive Event and History," *EOTH*, 314-335. Significant for our discussion are the following contributions of Pannenberg: "Kerygma und Geschichte," *Studien zur Theologie der alttestamentlichen Überlieferungen*, ed. R. Rendtorff und K. Koch (Neukirchen, 1961), pp. 129-140 (hereafter cited as *Studien*); Pannenberg, ed., *Offenbarung als Geschichte* (2nd ed.; Göttingen, 1963; hereafter cited as *OaG*); this appeared in English as *Revelation as History* (New York, 1968); Pannenberg, *Jesus — God and Man* (Philadelphia, 1968); *Grundfragen systematischer Theologie* (Göttingen, 1968). Noteworthy critiques of Pannenberg and his group are by Hans-Georg Geyer, "Geschichte als theologisches Problem," *EvTh*, 22 (1962), 92-104; Lothar Steiger, "Offenbarungsgeschichte und theologische Vernunft," *ZThK*, 59 (1962), 88-113; Günther Klein, "Offenbarung als Geschichte?" *Monatsschrift für Pastoraltheologie*, 51 (1962), 65-88, to which Pannenberg replied in the "Postscript" of the 2nd ed. of *OaG*, pp. 132-148; Klein, *Theologie des Wortes Gottes und die Hypothese der Universalgeschichte. Zur Auseinandersetzung mit Wolfhart Pannenberg* (Beiträge zur Evangelischen Theologie, 37; München, 1964); Hesse, "Wolfhart Pannenberg und das AT," *Neue Zeitschrift für systematische Theologie und Religionswissenschaft*, 7 (1965), 174-199; Gerhard Sauter, *Zukunft und Verheissung. Das Problem der Zukunft in der gegenwärtigen theologischen und philosophischen Diskussion* (Zürich/Stuttgart, 1965), pp. 239-251; R. L. Wilken, "Who Is Wolfhart Pannenberg?" *Dialogue*, 4 (1965), 140-142; D. P. Fuller, "A New German Theological Movement," *Scottish Journal of Theology*, 19 (1966), 160-175; G. G. O'Collins, "Revelation as History," *Heythrop Journal*, 7 (1966), 394-406; R. T. Osborn, "Pannenberg's Programme," *Canadian Journal of Theology*, 13 (1967), 109-122; H. Obay-

presupposition for his entire theological program seems to lie in his understanding of history as "reality in its totality."[61] History is encompassing man's past and present reality.[62] He traces the development of this concept of history as "reality in its totality" from ancient Israel to the present. Pannenberg argues against the common distinction between historical facts and their meaning, evaluation, and interpretation by man. He feels that this common procedure in modern historiography is a result of the influence of positivism and neo-Kantianism. Pannenberg proposes that against such an artificial distinction "we must reinstate today the original unity of facts and their meaning."[63] That is to say that "in principle, every event has its original meaning within the context of occurrence and tradition in which it took place. . . ."[64] Pannenberg's objective, in light of this analysis, is to create a situation in which faith can rest on historically proven fact in order to be saved from subjectivity, self-redemption, and self-deception.[65]

Pannenberg emphasizes the thesis of "revelation as history."[66] The goal of "Yahweh's action in history is that he be known — revelation. His action . . . aims at the goal that Yahweh will be revealed in his action as he fulfills his vow."[67] The connection between the Testaments is constituted by the one history, namely universal history,

ashi, "Pannenberg and Troeltsch: History and Religion," *Journal of the American Academy of Religion*, 38 (1970), 401-419.

[61] *EOTH*, p. 319.

[62] Pannenberg, *Grundfragen systematischer Theologie*, p. 391.

[63] *Supra*, n. 55.

[64] Pannenberg, *Theology as History*, p. 127.

[65] P. 269: "The knowledge of history on which faith is grounded has to do with the truth and reliability of that on which faith depends; these are presupposed in the act of trusting, and thus logically precede the act of faith in respect to its perceived content. But that does not mean that the subjective accomplishment of such knowledge would be in any way a condition for participating in salvation, but rather it assures faith about its basis."

[66] This is the title of the collection of programmatic essays in *Revelation as History* (New York, 1968).

[67] *EOTH*, p. 317.

"which is itself grounded in the unity of the God who works here as well as there and remains true to his promises."[68] In universal history "the destiny of mankind, from creation onward, is seen to be unfolding according to a plan of God."[69] Thus he broadens salvation history (*Heilsgeschichte*) and makes it identical with universal history.[70] When "reality in its totality"[71] is conceived as universal history there would be nothing that can be excluded from this totality. Thus God's revelation is the inherent meaning of history, not something that is superadded to history.[72]

Whereas von Rad leaves open the relation of salvation history to history, Pannenberg, in his unified view of universal history, draws salvation history into his large category of universal history. Thus it seems impossible to maintain a radical disjunction between the two pictures of Israel's history, or between the past and the present or the present and the future. Thus Pannenberg enlarges the modern concept of history to include the totality of reality into the historical-critical method, which by definition had limited itself. Pannenberg's whole theology seems to fly away from radical historicalness of the present to contemplation of the whole. H. Obayashi says that Pannenberg's understanding of history as the totality of reality, despite its allegedly historical character, takes "off from the classical ontological question and settles it in an ontological end of time."[73] "If *Heilsgeschichte* theology had fled from history to some safe harbor, Pannenberg departed from that harbor and re-entered history only to find in the nature of history, which is immense and inexhaustible, a self-con-

68 P. 329.

69 Pannenberg, *Revelation as History*, p. 132.

70 P. 133.

71 *EOTH*, p. 319.

72 *Revelation as History*, p. 136.

73 Obayashi, p. 405; cf. W. Hamilton, "Character of Pannenberg's Theology," *Theology as History*, p. 178.

tained totality in which the end plays an overwhelming role that immunizes the significance of the present."[74]

On the positive side it must be emphasized that Pannenberg seeks to take a firm stand on the transcendent reality which E. Troeltsch held in abeyance and relegated to personal choice.[75] For Pannenberg a transcendent reality is presupposed in man's openness and structure of existence.[76] Pannenberg's critique of Troeltsch's historical method, of which the principle of analogy is based upon a one-sided anthropocentric presupposition, is to the point.[77] Pannenberg works with a synthetic historical-critical method which emphasizes the original unity of facts and their meaning and a methodological anthropocentrism which is said to be capable of including the realm of the transcendent within its own presupposition.[78]

Rolf Rendtorff,[79] a member of Pannenberg's "working circle" with Ulrich Wilckens[80] and Dietrich Rössler,[81] proposes to relate salvation history to the historical-critical picture of Israel's history. He would combine what

[74] P. 413.

[75] E. Troeltsch, *Gesammelte Schriften* (Tübingen, 1922), III, 657ff.

[76] *Grundfragen systematischer Theologie*, pp. 283f.

[77] Pannenberg, "Heilsgeschehen und Geschichte," *Grundfragen systematischer Theologie*, pp. 46-54; cf. Obayashi, pp. 407f.

[78] *Grundfragen systematischer Theologie*, p. 54.

[79] Rendtorff is the OT theologian of the group, of whose writings the following are important for the issue at hand: "Hermeneutik des AT als Frage nach der Geschichte," *ZThK*, 57 (1960), 27-40; "Die Offenbarungsvorstellungen im alten Israel," *OaG*, pp. 21-41; "Die Entstehung der israelitischen Religion als religionsgeschichtliches und theologisches Problem," *ThLZ*, 88 (1963), cols. 735-746; "Alttestamentliche Theologie und israelitisch-jüdische Religionsgeschichte," *Zwischenstation. Festschrift für Karl Kupisch zum 60. Geburtstag*, ed. Helmut Gollwitzer and J. Hoppe (München, 1963), pp. 208-222. Noteworthy also is the critique of Rendtorff by Arnold Gamper, "Offenbarung in Geschichte," *ZThK*, 86 (1964), 180-196.

[80] "Das Offenbarungsverständnis in der Geschichte des Urchristentums," *OaG*, pp. 42-90.

[81] D. Rössler, *Gesetz und Geschichte. Untersuchungen zur Theologie der jüdischen Apokalyptik und der pharisäischen Orthodoxie* (*WMANT*, 3; 2nd ed.; Neukirchen, 1962).

is currently separated into "history of Israel," "history of tradition," and "OT theology" into one new genre of scholarly research. Since this is all united in the tradition, he elevates the term "tradition" to the center of his discussion. He explains that "Israel's history takes place in the external events which are commonly the subject of historical-critical research of history *and* in the manifold and stratified inner events, which we have gathered under the term tradition."[82] Therefore, the historical-critical method is to be transformed and extended so as to be able to verify at the same time God's revelation in history. It is not surprising that Rendtorff has much to say about the relation of word and event. He is of the conviction that "word has an essential part in the event of revelation." But this should not be understood to mean that word has priority over event. Quite on the contrary, the word does not need to be the mediator between the event and the one who experiences the event, because "the event itself can and should bring about a recognition of Yahweh in the one who sees it and understands it to be the act of Yahweh."[83]

But apart from employing the term "tradition" in his comprehensive horizon, Rendtorff's attempt does not go beyond von Rad, who even used it in the subtitles of his two volumes on OT theology. It needs to be asked what kind of relevance one can expect of the tradition history. Undoubtedly the history of tradition is able to further Biblical-theological expounding and interpretation, but the question remains whether or not this method, even in a broadened perspective, can be made the "canon" of Biblical-theological understanding. H.-J. Kraus remarks critically that "the strange optimism, believing

[82] Rendtorff, *Studien*, p. 84.

[83] *OaG*, p. 40. Zimmerli countered Rendtorff in " 'Offenbarung' im AT," *EvTh*, 22 (1962), 15-31, to which Rendtorff replied with "Geschichte und Wort im AT," *EvTh*, 22 (1962), 621-649. A summary of the debate is given by Robinson, "Revelation as Word and as History," *Theology as History*, pp. 42-62.

that with the wonder word 'history of tradition' both
faith and history can be handled, leads of necessity to
the security of the program 'revelation as history'."[84]

In view of this situation Kraus has correctly pointed
out that "one of the most difficult questions of the laying
hold of and presenting of 'Biblical theology' is that of
the starting-point, the meaning and function of historical-critical research."[85] Von Rad's theology is in its starting-point definitely a historical-critical undertaking,
as is evident in that his theology is a theology of traditions. This approach contains many questions. One crucial problem area is the relationship of history of tradition and salvation history. Let me illustrate what I mean.
The prophets of Israel actualized the ancient traditions;
the old was made new. Among them "a critical way of
thinking sprang up which learned how to select, combine, and even reject, data from the wealth of tradition. . . ."[86] This whole process von Rad calls a "charis-
matic-eclectic process."[87] What about this "process" out
of which a "linear course of history"[88] was constructed
which in turn produced new historical events? The question that arises is whether or not the Biblical event is
traditio-historical event. Or to express it differently, Is
the horizontal structural framework of the traditions the
decisive "process" which an OT theology has to adopt
and to explicate? Is the theology of the history of traditions properly OT theology? The aim of these critical
questions is not to minimize the right and meaning of
traditio-historical research. Yet one cannot shirk the responsibility to come to grips with the question whether
or not OT theology has its methodological starting-point
in the traditio-historical method. To speak with Kraus,

[84] *Die Biblische Theologie*, p. 370.
[85] P. 363.
[86] *TAT*, II, 118; *OTT*, II, 108.
[87] *TAT*, II, 345. Cf. Baumgärtel, *ThLZ*, 12 (1961), 901-903.
[88] *TAT*, II, 118; *OTT*, II, 108.

it seems that OT theology is only theology of the OT[89] in that it "accepts the given textual context as contained in the canon as *historical truth* whose final form is in need of explanation and interpretation in a summary presentation."[90] If this is the proper task of OT theology, then it is not to be considered a "history of revelation," "history of religion," or "history of tradition" as the case may be.[91]

In the present writer's opinion it seems feasible neither to ground "salvation history" in the historical-critical method (Hesse) nor to enlarge the historical-critical method to such an extent that the totality of reality can come to expression through it (Pannenberg, Rendtorff), because the major presuppositional and philosophical adjustments to be made would so radically change this method that its historical-critical nature as commonly understood at present would be obliterated. Nevertheless, no matter how we evaluate the way in which Pannenberg and his group worked out their theologies, Pannenberg's proposal that "we must reinstate today the original unity of facts and their meaning"[92] calls for serious consideration as a new starting-point for overcoming the modern dichotomy by which historiography has wrenched apart the history of Israel under such outmoded and questionable influences as positivism and

[89] Ebeling, *Word and Faith,* pp. 79f., points up the ambiguity of the term Biblical theology, which can mean either the theology contained in the Bible or the theology that has Biblical character and accords with the Bible. The same distinction is applicable to OT theology. OT theology means the theology contained in the OT, and this theology has also normative claims.

[90] *Die Biblische Theologie,* p. 364 (italics his).

[91] Vriezen, *An Outline of OT Theology²,* pp. 146f.; and also Kraus, *Die Biblische Theologie,* pp. 364f. Kraus goes on to explain that this is not a new Biblicism but a part of the critical theological task to continue to test and explain methodological procedures.

[92] Pannenberg, *Theology as History,* p. 127.

neo-Kantianism.[93] Faith would thus not be established by the "language of facts"[94] nor by any proof of events on the basis of the historical-critical method, but by the fact of language, which brings both event and word as a central original unity to the hearer. Thus when we speak of God's acts in Israel's history, there is no reason to confine this activity to a few bare events, *bruta facta*, that the schema of historical criticism can verify by cross-checking with other historical evidences. Nor is it adequate and appropriate to employ the hermeneutical schema of von Rad, because with neither schema has scholarship been able to reach a fully acceptable understanding of historical reality, due to serious methodological, historical, and theological limitations, restrictions, and inadequacies. God's acts are with the totality of Israel's career in history, including the highly complex and diverse ways in which she developed and transmitted her confessions. Thus we must work with a method that takes account of the totality of that history under the recognition of the original unity of facts and their meaning and an adequate concept of total reality.

[93] The OT theologian Christoph Barth argues in "Grundprobleme einer Theologie des AT," *EvTh*, 23 (1963), 368, against a critical methodology that declares every "suprahuman and supranatural causality" unhistorical, as well as against a "rational-objective method" that believes itself able to distinguish without great difficulty between "real" and "interpreted" history.

[94] Pannenberg, *OaG,* pp. 100, 112.

III. The Center of the OT and OT Theology

The question whether the OT has something that can be considered its center (German *Mitte*) is of considerable importance for its understanding and for doing OT theology. The matter of the center plays an important and at times even decisive role for presentations of OT theology.

It is not necessary to survey the development of this question during the last two centuries in which rather divergent presentations of Biblical theology were brought forth.[1] With the publication of Eichrodt's theology this question has come into new focus. For him the "central concept" and "covenient symbol"[2] for securing the unity of Biblical faith is the "covenant." "The concept of the covenant," explains Eichrodt, "was given this central position in the religious thinking of the OT so that, by working outward from it, the structural unity of the OT message might be made more readily visible."[3] He does not consider it a "doctrinal concept, with the help of which a complete corpus of dogma can be worked out, but the characteristic *description of a living process*, which was begun at a particular time and at a

[1] We would like to draw attention to the short recent study of the subject by R. Smend, *Die Mitte des AT* (Zürich, 1970), pp. 7, 27-33.
[2] *TOT*, I, 13f.
[3] *TOT*, I, 17.

49

particular place, in order to reveal a divine reality unique in the whole history of religion."[4] Thus Eichrodt's theology represents one of the most impressive attempts to understand the OT as a whole not only from a center but from the unifying concept "covenant."

It appears that the discoveries of the legal background of the Mosaic covenant as particularly stimulated by G. E. Mendenhall[5] further undergird Eichrodt's emphasis. The ensuing discussion, however, has somewhat dampened the early enthusiasm.[6] Now G. Fohrer even thinks that the covenant between Yahweh and Israel played no role at all in Israel between the end of the 13th and the end of the 7th century B.C.,[7] a point to which Eichrodt has responded[8] and in which Fohrer may see things from

[4] *TOT*, I, 14 (italics his). The centrality of the covenant for OT religion has found supporters long before Eichrodt: August Kayser, *Die Theologie des AT in ihrer geschichtlichen Entwicklung dargestellt* (Strassburg, 1886), p. 74: "Der Alles beherrschende Gedanke der Propheten, der Schwer- und Stützpunkt der alttestamentlichen Religion überhaupt, ist die Idee der Theokratie, oder, um den im A.T. üblichen Ausdruck zu gebrauchen, die Idee des Bundes." G. F. Oehler, *Theologie des AT* (Tübingen, 1873), I, 69: "Die Grundlage der alttestamentlichen Religion bildet der Bund in welchen Gott zur Verwirklichung seines Heilsraths mit dem erwählten Stamm getreten ist."

[5] *Law and Covenant in Israel and the Ancient East* (Pittsburgh, 1955); "Covenant," *IDB*, I, 714-723.

[6] For a summary of the discussion, see D. J. McCarthy, "Covenant in the OT: The Present State of Inquiry," *CBQ*, 27 (1965), 217-240; *Der Gottesbund im AT* (2nd ed.; Stuttgart, 1967). The latter contains a comprehensive bibliography.

[7] "AT —'Amphiktyonie' und 'Bund'?" *ThLZ*, 91 (1966), 893-904; "Der Mittelpunkt einer Theologie des AT," *ThZ*, 24 (1968), 162f. L. Perlitt, *Bundestheologie im AT* (WMANT, 36; Neukirchen-Vluyn, 1971), believes that the covenant theology in the OT is a late fruit of Israelite belief which is due to the theological creativity of the Deuteronomistic movement and epoch. This then explains the "covenant silence" in the prophets of the 8th century.

[8] W. Eichrodt, "Prophet and Covenant: Observations on the Exegesis of Isaiah," *Proclamation and Presence: OT Essays in Honor of G. Henton Davies*, ed. J. I. Durham and J. R. Porter (Richmond, 1970), pp. 167-188, maintains that the original covenant of Yahweh with Israel is not mentioned by Isaiah because the prophet did not wish to argue about a concept that was so important in his own faith. On the whole question, see R. E. Clements, *Prophecy and Covenant* (*SBT*, 43; London, 1965).

a too limited perspective. The importance of the covenant motif in the OT is not to be denied, but the crucial
question remains: Is the covenant concept broad enough
to include adequately within its grasp the totality of OT
reality? One cannot but give a negative answer to the
question. The problem remains whether or not any single
concept should or can be employed for bringing about
a "structural unity of the OT message" when the OT
message resists from within such systematization.

Various scholars have felt that the OT has other cen-
ters. E. Sellin chooses as the central idea to guide him
in his exposition of OT theology the holiness of God.
"It is that which characterizes the deepest and inner-
most nature of the OT God."[9] Sellin makes the point that
his OT theology is interested "only in the single great
line which has found its completion in the Gospel, the
word of the eternal God in the OT writings."[10] Whereas
the national-cultic religion of popular belief looks mainly
to the past and present, the ethical and universal religion
of the prophets looks to the future, to the coming of the
Holy One in judgment and salvation both of which arise
out of the holiness of God.[11]

Like Eichrodt and Sellin, Ludwig Köhler has his own
favorite central concept, namely that of God as the
Lord.[12] For Köhler the fundamental and determining
assertion of OT theology should be that God is the Lord.
"This statement is the backbone of Old Testament theology."[13] The rulership and kingship of God are merely
corollaries to God's lordship.[14]

Hans Wildberger suggests that "the central concept of
the OT is Israel's election as the people of God."[15] Horst

9 *Theologie des AT* (2nd ed.; Leipzig, 1936), p. 19.
10 P. 1.
11 Pp. 21-23.
12 *OT Theology*, trans. A. S. Todd (Philadelphia, 1957), p. 30.
13 P. 35.
14 P. 31.
15 "Auf dem Wege zu einer biblischen Theologie," *EvTh,* 19 (1959),
77f.

Seebass stresses the "rulership of God."[16] Günther Klein argues for the "kingdom of God as a central concept"[17] in both OT and NT. Georg Fohrer answers the question of the OT "from which it can proceed and around which everything can be grouped"[18] with a "dual concept,"[19] "namely the *rule* of God and the *communion* between God and man."[20] These two poles belong together as the two foci of an ellipse.[21] They "constitute the unifying element in the manifoldedness"[22] of the theological expressions and movements in the OT from which a Biblical theology of both OT and NT can be constructed. The OT and NT are then not to be correlated in terms of promise and fulfillment or failure and realization, but "in the relationship of beginning and continuation [*Beginn und Fortsetzung*]."[23] With the aid of this dual center and on the basis of this twofold relationship the OT does not need to be devaluated or reinterpreted but it can be taken seriously in its own uniqueness.

The thoroughly revised and rewritten new edition of Vriezen's theology is related at least in one key aspect to the views of Fohrer. Although Vriezen explicitly affirms that God "is the *focal point* of all the Old Testament writings" and stoutly maintains that "Old Testament theology must *centre* upon Israel's God as the God of the Old Testament in His relations to the people, man,

[16]"Der Beitrag des AT zum Entwurf einer biblischen Theologie," *Wort und Dienst,* 8 (1965), 34-42.

[17]"'Reich Gottes' als biblischer Zentralbegriff," *EvTh,* 30 (1970), 642-670.

[18]"The Centre of a Theology of the OT," *Nederduitse Gereformeerde Theologiese Tydskrift,* 7 (1966), 198; the same article appeared in German, with footnotes, under the title, "Der Mittelpunkt einer Theologie des AT," *ThZ,* 24 (1968), 161.

[19]"Das AT und das Thema 'Christologie'," *EvTh,* 30 (1970), 295: "Denn bei der Frage nach einem Mittelpunkt der alttestamentlichen Theologie ergibt sich die Doppelvorstellung der Herrschaft Gottes und der Gemeinschaft zwischen Gott und Mensch."

[20]*ThZ,* 24 (1968), 163 (italics his).

[21]*EvTh,* 30 (1970), 295.

[22]*ThZ,* 24 (1968), 163; *EvTh,* 30 (1970), 295.

[23]*ThZ,* 24 (1968), 163.

and the world. . . ,"[24] one must clearly understand that
the central element for his structure of OT theology is
the concept of "communion."[25] Vriezen calls the communion concept the "underlying idea," "essential root
idea,"[26] "fundamental idea,"[27] or "keystone,"[28] of the
message of the OT. Why does he prefer the communion
concept above the covenant concept as used by Eichrodt? Vriezen believes that the covenant did not bring
the two covenant partners "into contract-relation, but
into a communion, with God. . . ."[29] He adds that "we
cannot be certain that the communion between God and
the people was considered from the outset as a *cove-
nantal* communion."[30] Since the NT is in Vriezen's view,
shared also by Fohrer,[31] in complete agreement with the
OT in that communion is the "fundamental point of
faith," it follows for Vriezen that the fundamental idea
of "communion between God and man is the best starting-point for a Biblical theology of the Old Testament,"
which must "be arranged with this aspect in view."[32]
Thus it turns out that Vriezen's newest attempt is a
combination of the cross-section and his confessional
methods. The similarity between Eichrodt's OT theology
and that of Vriezen is that both work with complementary methodologies. The difference between the two
scholars lies in that Eichrodt employs his type of cross-
section method with the use of the covenant concept
but remaining with both feet planted in history. Eichrodt is thus more descriptive and Vriezen more confes-

[24] *An Outline of OT Theology*[2], p. 150 (italics mine).
[25] P. 8, where Vriezen writes that the main part of his book (chs. 6-11)
has undergone an important transformation in form since he "attempted
to establish the 'communion' . . . as the centre of all the expositions."
[26] P. 160.
[27] P. 170.
[28] P. 164.
[29] P. 169.
[30] P. 351.
[31] *EvTh*, 30 (1970), 296-298.
[32] *An Outline of OT Theology*[2], p. 175.

sional. The latter achieves structural unity with the aid of the single communion concept.

Rudolf Smend's recent study on the center of the OT revives Wellhausen's formula, "Yahweh the God of Israel, Israel the people of Yahweh."[33] If this particularistic formula is accepted, argues Smend, then the tension between God and Israel can come to expression in an OT theology. At this point it is significant to note that Smend, as Fohrer before him, recognizes that a single concept is unable to do justice to the manifold and multiform testimony of the OT. He would, therefore, choose this formula rather than a single concept because with this formula one is able to come to grips with a significant tension in the OT. But Smend himself admits that this formula does not express the center of the whole OT and is decidedly of limited value with regard to the Christian Scriptural canon of OT and NT.[34] Aside from the latter point, however, this formula would seem too particularistic, for within the tension between Yahweh and his people with which this formula is concerned one is unable to expound the universalistic emphasis of the OT, i.e., Yahweh's action with the world and the world vis-à-vis Yahweh. Yahweh is not only the God of Israel but also the Lord of the world.[35]

[33]*Die Mitte des AT*, pp. 49, 55. J. Wellhausen, *Israelitisch-jüdische Religion. Die Kultur der Gegenwart I/4:1* (Leipzig, 1905), p. 8, states that the sentence "Yahweh the God of Israel and Israel the people of Yahweh" has "been for all times the short essence of the Israelite religion." Bernhard Duhm, *Die Theologie der Propheten* (Leipzig, 1875), p. 96, has argued that in the dual formula "Israel, Yahweh's people and Yahweh, Israel's God" the "whole content of prophetic religion has come fully to expression." B. Stade, *Biblische Theologie des AT* (2nd ed.; Tübingen, 1905), I, 31, holds that "Yahweh, Israel's God" is "the basic idea of the religion of Israel." Martin Noth, *Die israelitischen Personennamen im Rahmen der gemeinsemitischen Namengebung* (2nd ed.; Hildesheim, 1966), p. 81, believes that in the "sentence, that expresses that Yahweh is Israel's God and Israel is Yahweh's people" comes to expression the "characteristic nature" of Israelite religion.

[34]*Die Mitte des AT*, pp. 55-58.

[35]Seebass, *Wort und Dienst*, 8 (1965), 38-41, speaks of Yahweh as a "Weltherrschergott."

Smend argues that the OT should be studied on the basis of its center.[36] Against this principle there is hardly any sound objection to be advanced. But one needs to be on guard that one does not yield to the temptation to make a single concept or a certain formula into an abstract divining-rod with which all OT expressions and testimonies are combined into a unified system. Though Smend is aware of this danger, he nevertheless makes such a definite use of his particularistic formula that it turns out to serve as *the* key for the systematic ordering of the OT materials, subjects, themes, and motifs.[37] This goes beyond the limits that must be imposed upon the usage and significance of a center of the OT whatever it may be. One must always be on guard not to overstep the boundaries inherent in any kind of center. K. H. Miskotte has correctly warned that a center should not turn out "to become the timelessly gesticulative content of the Old Testament."[38] Each of the suggestions so far described has undoubtedly much in its favor. At the same time every one of them seems to be wanting. They fall short because they try to grasp the OT in terms of a single basic concept or limited formula through which the OT message in its manifoldness and variety, its continuity and discontinuity, is ordered, arranged and systematized when the multiplex and multiform nature of the OT resists such handling of its materials and thoughts.

Here Gerhard von Rad's absolute No to the question of the center of the OT in its relation to the doing of OT theology has a unique significance. Von Rad's position merits a more detailed analysis, since he claims unequivocally that "on the basis of the Old Testament itself, it is truly difficult to answer the question of the unity of that Testament, for it has no focal-point [*Mitte*]

[36] *Die Mitte des AT,* p. 49.

[37] Pp. 54f.

[38] *Wenn die Götter schweigen. Vom Sinn des AT* (3rd ed.; München, 1966), p. 127.

as is found in the New Testament."[39] Whereas the NT
has Jesus Christ as its center, the OT lacks such a center.[40] Yahweh as the center of the OT "would not be
sufficient."[41] Why? "Unlike the revelation in Christ, the
revelation of Jahweh in the Old Testament is divided up
over a long series of separate acts of revelation which
are very different in content. It seems to be without a
centre which determines everything and which could
give to the various separate acts both an interpretation
and their proper theological connection with one another."[42] The later von Rad is less rigid in his denial of
a center of the OT. He actually admits that "one can
say, Yahweh is the center of the Old Testament."[43] "God
stood at the center," says von Rad, "of the (theologically
rather flexible) conception of history of the writers of
ancient Israelite history."[44] Nevertheless this is where
the question begins for von Rad: "What kind of Yahweh

[39] TAT, II, 376; OTT, II, 362. Earlier von Rad, "Kritische Vor-
arbeiten zu einer Theologie des AT," Theologie und Liturgie, ed. L.
Hennig (München, 1952), p. 30, stated the following: "So müssen wir
uns wohl noch bewusster und konsequenter dem uns im Grunde un-
heimlichen Phänomen der Mittelosigkeit des AT stellen. An die Stelle
der Mitte tritt der Weg oder wie Jesaja es für das alttestamentliche
Ganze gültig formuliert hat, das 'Werk' Jahwehs (Jes. 5, 15. 19; 10, 12;
22, 12)." ThLZ, 88 (1963), col. 405 n. 3a: "Was hat es überhaupt mit dieser
fast unisono gestellten Frage nach der 'Einheit,' der 'Mitte' des AT auf
sich? Ist das etwas so Selbstverständliches, dass ihr Aufweis sozusagen
zu conditio sine qua non einer ordentlichen Theologie des AT gehört?
Und auf welcher Ebene soll sich diese (von vorneherein als vorhanden
akzeptierte) Einheit aufweisen lassen, auf dem Gebiet der geschichtlichen
Erfahrungen Israels oder in seiner Gedankenwelt? Oder handelt es sich
bei diesem Postulat weniger um ein Anliegen der historischen oder
theologischen Erkenntnis als um ein spekulativ-philosophisches Prinzip,
das als bewusste Prämisse wirksam wird?"

[40] TAT, II, 376f.; OTT, II, 362.

[41] OTT, II, 362f.

[42] TAT, I, 128; OTT, I, 115. On the other hand, on the same page
we find that von Rad claims that OT theology has "its starting point
and its centre . . . [in] Jahweh's action in revelation."

[43] ThLZ, 88 (1963), 406. Vriezen, An Outline of OT Theology[2], p. 150
n. 4, seems to go astray when he implies that von Rad may make Christ
the center of the OT.

[44] ThLZ, 88 (1963), 409.

after all is this?"[45] Is it one who hides himself more and more in every act of self-revelation? This question can be answered best by von Rad's own methodological procedure.

Von Rad proceeds from a kind of secret center, which reveals itself in his basic thesis, namely that the establishment of God's self-revelation takes place in his acts in history: "History is the place in which God reveals the secret of his person."[46] With this thesis von Rad has won a "heuristic measuring rod"[47] with which all statements, all witnesses of faith of the OT, are measured as to their theological relevance and legitimacy.

Von Rad is very emphatic to point out that the OT is not a book that gives an account of historical facts as they "really happened." He states: "The Old Testament is a history book [Geschichtsbuch]; it tells of God's history with Israel, with the nations, and with the world, from the creation of the world down to the last things, that is to say, down to the time when dominion over the world is given to the Son of Man (Dan. VII. 13f.)."[48] Already the earliest confessions (the Credo of Deut. 26) were historically determined, i.e., "they connect the name of this God with some statement about an action in history." Von Rad explains, "This history can be described as saving history [Heilsgeschichte] because, as it is presented, creation itself is understood as a saving act of God and because, according to what the prophets

[45] Col. 406.

[46] I have supplied my own translation of this key sentence from TAT, II, 349: "Der Ort, an dem Gott sein Personengeheimnis offenbart, ist die Geschichte." In the translation of OTT, II, 338, part of its significance is lost: ". . . that it is in history that God reveals the secret of his person." Von Rad does not follow the usual distinction made in German between Historie and Geschichte. He employs the term Geschichte almost to the complete exclusion of Historie, which according to the index is used only once, TAT, II, 8.

[47] This phrase stems from Martin Honecker, "Zum Verständnis der Geschichte in Gerhard von Rads Theologie des AT," EvTh, 23 (1963), 145.

[48] TAT, II, 370; OTT, II, 415.

foretold, God's will to save is, in spite of many acts of judgment, to achieve its goal."[49] As a result of this view the Psalms and Wisdom literature of the OT are accorded the position of "Israel's answer"[50] to the early experiences of Israel with Yahweh. The OT prophets, on the other hand, are not reformers with a message of an entirely new kind. "Instead, they regarded themselves as the spokesmen of old and well-known sacral traditions which they reinterpreted for their own day and age."[51] Thus it becomes apparent that von Rad employs his understanding of OT history as a hermeneutical schema for interpreting the OT. The type of history of which von Rad speaks finds its clearest formulation in the Deuteronomist, whose view of history is described in the following way: "The history of Israel is a course of events [*Zeitablauf*] which received its own peculiar dramatic quality from the tension between constantly promulgated prophecies and their corresponding fulfilment."[52] This explains why in von Rad's OT theology cultic and wisdom elements recede,[53] for his view of history is interested neither in secular history nor in the history of faith and cult, but is concerned solely "with the problem of how the word of Jahweh functioned in history."[54] Fundamentally expressed, this means that the "Deuteronomistic theology of history was the first which clearly formulated the phenomenon of saving history, that is, of a course of history which was shaped and led to a fulfilment by a word of judgment and salvation continually injected into it."[55]

The prophetic message is by von Rad likewise interpreted from this center, namely the Deuteronomistic

49 *TAT*, II, 370f.; *OTT*, II, 357f.
50 *TAT*, I, 366ff.; *OTT*, I, 355ff.
51 *TAT*, II, 185; *OTT*, II, 175.
52 *TAT*, I,   352; *OTT*, I, 340.
53 Honecker, p. 146.
54 *TAT*, I, 354; *OTT*, I, 343.
55 *TAT*, I, 356; *OTT*, I, 344.

theology of history.[56] Accordingly one of the greatest achievements of prophecy "was to recapture for faith the dimension in which Jahweh had revealed himself par excellence, that of history and politics."[57] The essential step of the prophets beyond the tradition of salvation history handed down to them, which was oriented in the past, consists in their opening the future as the place of the action of God.[58] This projection of God's acts to the future, which is felt to be an "eschatologizing of concepts of history,"[59] takes up the old confessional traditions and places them with the help of "creative interpretation"[60] within the horizon of a new saving event. "Projecting the old traditions into the future was the only possible way open to the prophets of making material statements about a future which involved God."[61] The eschatological character of the prophetic message consists of a negation of the old historical bases of salvation, and in that it does not remain with past historical acts, it "suddenly shifted the basis of salvation to a future action of God."[62] The kerygma of the prophets thus takes place within tensions created by three factors: "the new eschatological word with which Jahweh addresses Israel, the old election tradition, and the personal situation, be it one which incurred penalty or one which needed comfort, of the people addressed by the prophet."[63]

[56] The problem of this one-sided interpretation of prophecy is apparently known to von Rad, since he points to the question of how far the prophet was "a spiritual man who stood in direct religious relationship to God" and a proclaimer of "the universal moral order." "In all probability, the questions considered by earlier criticism will one day require to be taken up again, though under different theological presuppositions" (*TAT*, II, 311; *OTT*, II, 298).

[57] *TAT*, II, 192; *OTT*, II, 182.
[58] *TAT*, II, 129ff.; *OTT*, II, 115ff.
[59] *TAT*, II, 125ff.; *OTT*, II, 112ff.
[60] *TAT*, II, 313; *OTT*, II, 300.
[61] *TAT*, II, 312; *OTT*, II, 299.
[62] *TAT*, II, 131; *OTT*, II, 118.
[63] *TAT*, II, 140; *OTT*, II, 130.

In short, von Rad gains his understanding of history
from the Deuteronomistic theology of history according
to which salvation history is led to its goal, its fulfillment,
by means of the word of Yahweh. This seems surprising
if one considers that von Rad's research had its starting-point in the Hexateuch, from which it moved to the
prophets as the closing interpreters of the transmitted
events of salvation. The eschatologizing thought of
prophecy is, however, interpreted by von Rad on the
basis of the center as found in the Deuteronomistic theology of history and in this way it is bound to the primi-
tive *heilsgeschichtliche* confession. Thus von Rad intro-
duces into OT theology not only a historico-relational
concept but also a certain historico-theological center,
that of the theology of history of the Deuteronomistic
historian, as a determinative hermeneutical schema.

Parenthetically, we may point out that a complete discussion of von Rad's center as found in history should
include a treatment of his exposition of salvation history
as it moves in the tension between promise and fulfillment to be finally fully consummated in the Christ-event.
This would carry us, however, beyond the immediate
scope of the question at hand. For our purpose it will
suffice to point out that what is at work here is the interrelatedness of a twofold methodology: first, the "structural analogy," which consists of the "peculiar intercon-
nexion of revelation by word and revelation by event";[64]
and, secondly, "typological thinking," which is based not
"on myth and speculation, but on history and eschatology."[65] The questions that are raised by such a twofold
methodology cannot be treated at this point.[66] In short, we

[64] *TAT*, II, 376; *OTT*, II, 363; cf. the discussion of Hasel, "The
Problem of History in OT Theology," *AUSS*, 8 (1970), 32-35.

[65] *TAT*, II, 378; *OTT*, II, 365.

[66] For these questions see Hans Walter Wolff, "Zur Hermeneutik des
AT," *EvTh*, 16 (1956), 337-370; "The Hermeneutics of the OT," *EOTH*,
pp. 160-199; "Das Geschichtsverständnis der alttestamentlichen Prophetie," *EvTh*, 20 (1960), 218-235; "The Understanding of History in the
O. T. Prophets," *EOTH*, pp. 336-355; Walther Eichrodt, "Ist die typo-

must say that von Rad arrives at the crowning consumma-
tion of salvation history in the Christ-event as a result of
the combination of three conceptions: the center of Deuteronomistic history; the predominance of event over
word; and the interpretation of history from the movement along the line of tension between promise and
fulfillment.

As we have seen above, von Rad believes he has
found the center from which to unlock the OT in the
Deuteronomistic theology of history. This, in fact, is his
hermeneutical schema for the interpretation of the entire OT. He has, however, failed to justify the right to
use such a center as a hermeneutical key; that is, he has
been satisfied with the phenomenological utilization of
his center as a method for doing OT theology. One must
ask whether with the same right one could not use the
so-called Priestly schema for interpreting the OT or the
apocalyptic universalism of history of the Pannenberg
group?[67]

In a twofold way von Rad admits inadvertently to a
center in the OT. On the one hand, he himself operates
on the basis of a center, namely the Deuteronomistic
theology of history, and on the other, he concedes more
recently that it is right to say that "God stood at the
center of the (theologically rather flexible) conception
of history of the writers of ancient Israelite history."[68]

---

logische Exegese sachgemässe Exegese?" *VT Supplement*, IV (1957), 161-
180; "Is Typological Exegesis an Appropriate Method?" *EOTH*, pp. 224-
245; Jürgen Moltmann, "Exegese und Eschatologie in der Geschichte,"
EvTh, 22 (1962), 61 n. 75.

[67] Pannenberg speaks of the concept of the apocalyptic universalism
of history in terms of an "universalgeschichtliche Konzeption" and an
"universalgeschichtliches Schema," in *Kerygma und Dogma*, V (1959), 237,
and in his "Geschichtsverständnis der Apokalyptik," *OaG*, p. 107; cf. U.
Wilckens, *OaG*, pp. 53f.; and Rössler, *Gesetz und Geschichte*, pp. 111ff.
For a critique of Rössler, see Philipp Vielhauer, "Apocalypses and Related Studies: Introduction," Edgar Hennecke, *NT Apocrypha*, ed. Wilhelm Schneemelcher, trans. R. McL. Wilson (Philadelphia, 1965), pp.
581-607, esp. 593.

[68] Von Rad, *ThLZ*, 88 (1963), 409.

Thus it appears that von Rad's initial No to the question of the center of the OT is not so much directed against a center as such but against making such a center "a speculative-philosophical principle, which becomes operative as a conscious premise"[69] in the doing of OT theology. Here von Rad's caution is to be taken seriously even though he himself is in the last analysis unfaithful to his own warning cries. Nevertheless we are indebted to von Rad for inviting us to look for a center anew and to redefine its function more strictly. We should neither return to a stage of discussion before von Rad[70] nor should we bypass him, but we should go beyond him.

The question of the center of the OT demands of the Biblical theologian most careful consideration, because he cannot and must not use a concept, fundamental idea, or formula as a principle for the systematic ordering and arranging of the OT kerygmatic message and as a key that determines from the start how he will present the content of the OT testimony.

We ought to recognize, of course, that the question of the center of the OT is in actuality the question of the unity of the OT, which in itself is part of the larger questions of the relationship between the OT and NT. Every theologian who devotes himself specially to OT research has to inquire into the inner unity[71] and the center of the manifold and multiplex testimony of the OT. If we do not want to indulge in the errors referred to above, we need to remain on the broadest base. We need to choose a center that encompasses both the particularism and universalism of the OT. It must also not gloss over the

[69] Col. 405 n. 3a.

[70] This seems to be the case with Smend, *Die Mitte des AT*, pp. 49-55, in his revival of the formula of Wellhausen.

[71] Ebeling, *Word and Faith*, pp. 95f.: "In the theology of the Old or New Testament the theologian who devotes himself specially to Old or New Testament research has to give an inclusive account of his understanding of the Old or New Testament, i.e. above all of the theological problems that come of inquiring into the inner unity of the manifold testimony of the Old or New Testament."

manifoldness and variety in both continuity and discontinuity within the OT message. It seems to be a given fact that whereas the NT is clearly *christo*centric the OT is correspondingly *theo*centric. This means that the center of the OT which qualifies most adequately with respect to the foregoing discussion cannot be anything other than God. The *theo*centric nature of the OT testimony is abundantly testified to in theophanies and epiphanies[72] as well as in the testimonies of God's actions in deed and word in history.[73] God as the center of the OT is affirmed among others[74] more recently by F. Baumgärtel, H. Graf Reventlow, and E. Jacob.[75]

[72] Baumgärtel, *ThLZ*, 86 (1961), 896 n. 4; and especially Jörg Jeremias, *Theophanie* (*WMANT*, 10; Neukirchen-Vluyn, 1965); E. Pax, *EPIPHANEIA, Ein religionsgeschichtlicher Beitrag zur biblischen Theologie* (München, 1955).

[73] Jacob, *Grundfragen alttestamentlicher Theologie*, pp. 18-24.

[74] J. Lindblom, "Zur Frage der Eigenart der alttestamentlichen Religion," *Werden und Wesen des AT* (*Beihefte zur ZAW*, 66; Berlin, 1936), p. 131. A. Heschel, *Man Is Not Alone* (New York, 1951), p. 129; Miskotte, *Wenn die Götter schweigen*, p. 139.

[75] Reventlow, *ThZ*, 17 (1961), 96; Wright, *The OT and Theology*, p. 44; Jacob, *Grundfragen alttestamentlicher Theologie*, p. 18.

IV. The Relationship Between the Testaments

For every Christian theologian OT theology is and must remain a part of Biblical theology. Separate treatments of the theology of the OT and NT were produced ever since the year 1797 when the first *Theologie des alten Testaments* was published by Georg Lorenz Bauer. We are reminded anew by G. Ebeling that the Biblical theologian has to study the interconnection between the Testaments and "has to give an account of his understanding of the Bible as a whole, i.e. above all of the theological problems that come of inquiring into the inner unity of the manifold testimony of the Bible."[1] This raises the questions of continuity and discontinuity, of whether one reads uniquely from the OT to the NT or from the NT back into the OT, or reciprocally from the OT to the NT and the NT to the OT. Basic to the whole question is not merely an articulation of the theological problem of the interrelatedness between both Testaments but also an inquiry into the nature of this unity and disunity, whether it is one of language, thought-forms, or content. It is not necessary at this point to present a comprehensive sketch of the positions scholars

[1] *Word and Faith*, p. 96.

take currently on these problems.[2] We may limit ourselves to significant recent attempts which mirror the major positions.

Some scholars have posited the problem of the relationship between the Testaments by designating the OT in fact as a book of a non-Christian religion. It is the merit of Rudolf Bultmann to seek the connection between the Testaments in the factual course of Israel's history.[3] But Bultmann determines this connection in such a way that OT history is a history of failure. The application of the Lutheran law/gospel distinction[4] and a modern type of Christomonism[5] leads him to view the OT as a "miscarriage [*Scheitern*] of history" which only through this failure turns into a kind of promise.[6] "To the Christian faith the Old Testament is no longer revelation as it has been, and still is, for the Jews." To the Christian "the

[2] The following studies are especially concerned with this problem: A. A. van Ruler, *The Christian Church and the OT,* trans. G. W. Bromiley (Grand Rapids, 1971); S. Amsler, *L'AT dans l'église* (Neuchâtel, 1960); J. D. Smart, *The Interpretation of Scripture* (Philadelphia, 1961); P. Grelot, *Sens chrétien de l'AT* (Tournai, 1962); B. W. Anderson, ed., *The OT and Christian Faith* (New York, 1963; hereafter cited as *OTCF*); C. Westermann, *The OT and Jesus Christ* (Minneapolis, 1970); R. E. Murphy, "The Relationship Between the Testaments," *CBQ,* 26 (1964), 349-359; "Christian Understanding of the OT," *Theology Digest,* 18 (1970), 321f.; F. Hesse, *Das AT als Buch der Kirche* (Gütersloh, 1966); K. Schwarzwäller, *Das AT in Christus* (Zürich, 1966); "Das Verhältnis AT-NT im Lichte der gegenwärtigen Bestimmungen," *EvTh,* 29 (1969), 281-307; P. Benoit and R. E. Murphy, eds., *How Does the Christian Confront the OT?* (New York, 1967); A. H. J. Gunneweg, "Über die Prädikabilität alttestamentlicher Texte," *ZThK,* 65 (1968), 389-413; N. Lohfink, *The Christian Meaning of the OT* (Milwaukee, 1968); H.-D. Preuss, "Das AT in der Verkündigung der Kirche," *Deutsches Pfarrerblatt,* 63 (1968), 73-79; Kraus, *Die Biblische Theologie,* pp. 193-305. Additional bibliography can be derived from all these studies.

[3] Cf. Bultmann in *EOTH,* pp. 50-75, and in *OTCF,* pp. 8-35.

[4] *OTCF,* pp. 22-30.

[5] On this the critique of Wright, *The OT and Theology,* pp. 30-38, is especially relevant.

[6] Bultmann, *EOTH,* p. 73: ". . . the miscarriage of history actually amounts to a promise." See on this Barr, *Old and New in Interpretation,* pp. 162f.; "The OT and the New Crisis of Biblical Authority," *Interpretation,* 25 (1971), 30-32.

history of Israel is not history of revelation."[7] "Thus the Old Testament is the presupposition of the New"[8] and nothing more nor anything less. Bultmann argues for the complete theological discontinuity between the OT and NT. The relationship between both Testaments "is not theologically relevant at all."[9] Nonetheless this history has according to him a promissory character precisely because in the failure of the hopes centered around the covenant concept, in the failure of the rule of God and his people, it becomes clear that "the situation of the justified man arises only on the basis of this miscarriage [*Scheitern*]."[10] In answer to this position, Walther Zimmerli has rightly asked whether for the NT "the hopes and history of Israel are really only shattered." "Is there not fulfillment here, even in the midst of the shattering?" He recognizes clearly that the concept of failure or shattering becomes the means by which Bultmann is able "to elevate the Christ-message purely out of history in existential interpretation. . . ." Zimmerli suggests not without reason that the concept of a pure brokenness of Israel's history must of necessity lead to an unhistorical conception of the Christ-event, namely a "new Christ-myth."[11] He points out that an aspect of shattering is present even in the OT, where the prophets themselves bear witness to the freedom of Yahweh to "legitimately interpret his promise through his fulfillment, and the interpretation [by Yahweh] can be full of surprises even for the prophet himself."[12] W. Pannenberg notes that the reason Bultmann finds no continuity between the Testaments "is certainly connected with the fact that he does not begin with the promises and their structure which

---

[7] Bultmann, *EOTH*, p. 31.
[8] *OTCF*, p. 14.
[9] P. 13. Cf. Westermann's critique in *EOTH*, pp. 124-128.
[10] Bultmann, *EOTH*, p. 75.
[11] "Promise and Fulfillment," *EOTH*, pp. 118-120.
[12] P. 107.

for Israel were the foundation of history, . . . promises which thus endure precisely in change."[13]

The conviction of Friedrich Baumgärtel shares with Bultmann the emphasis of the discontinuity between the Testaments.[14] But Baumgärtel is not able to follow Bultmann's thesis of a total failure. He assumes an enduring "basic-promise [*Grundverheissung*]."[15] All the OT promises (*promissiones*) "really have no relevance for us"[16] except the timeless basic-promise (*promissum*) "I am the Lord your God."[17] He completely abandons the proof from prophecy as unacceptable to our historical consciousness. Beyond this Baumgärtel sees the meaning of the OT only in that its frustrated "salvation-disaster history" exemplifies the way of man under law. As such the OT contains a "witness of a religion outside the Gospel."[18] "Viewed historically it has another place than the Christian religion,"[19] for the OT "is a witness out of a non-Christian religion."[20] Here Baumgärtel comes close to the position of Bultmann in relating the Testaments to each other in terms of the Lutheran law/gospel dichotomy. Baumgärtel, therefore, maintains that the historicity of Jesus Christ is not grounded in the OT but solely in the Incarnation.[21] One comes to recognize how in such an approach "the historicity of Jesus Christ falls when the history of Israel falls."[22] C. Westermann points out that Baumgärtel ultimately admits "that the church

[13] Pannenberg, "Redemptive Event and History," *EOTH*, pp. 325f.

[14] F. Baumgärtel, *Verheissung. Zur Frage des evangelischen Verständnisses des Alten Testaments* (Gütersloh, 1952), p. 92.

[15] F. Baumgärtel, "The Hermeneutical Problem of the OT," *EOTH*, p. 151.

[16] P. 132.

[17] P. 151.

[18] P. 156.

[19] P. 135; cf. *ThLZ*, 86 (1961), 806.

[20] *EOTH*, p. 145.

[21] P. 156.

[22] Pannenberg, *EOTH*, p. 326.

could also live without the Old Testament."[23] Von Rad
attacks the unhistorical concept of "basic-promise" by
characterizing the separation of such a single promise
from particular historically realized promises and prophecies as a "presumptuous encroachment."[24]

Baumgärtel's former student Franz Hesse makes the
same basic reduction of the manifold promises to the
single basic-promise.[25] In the OT the promises failed.
This is due to the chastening hand of God that made
Israel harden their hearts. By turning God's word into
its opposite, it is a warning and a dialectical witness to
God's activity in Israel which culminates in Christ's
cross.[26] Hesse pronounces the sharpest theological strictures on the OT on the ground that certain historical
data supposedly do not fit the facts.[27] Therefore the OT
can have meaning for the Christian only in pointing him
toward the salvation which is found in the NT.[28] The
criticisms against Baumgärtel apply also to Hesse. It
will not do, as it happened again and again in the case
of F. D. E. Schleiermacher[29] and still happens with Baumgärtel[30] and Hesse,[31] to discuss the NT arguments of fulfillment of prophecy as nothing but an anti-Jewish apolo-
getic, relevant only to the NT period.[32] It is a mistake to
believe, as Bultmann does, that the meaning of the
"proof from Scripture" has as its purpose to "prove" what
can only be grasped by faith, or to approach and criticize

[23] "Remarks on the Theses of Bultmann and Baumgärtel," *EOTH*,
p. 133.
[24] "Verheissung," *EvTh*, 13 (1953), 410. See also the incisive criticism
against Baumgärtel by Gunneweg, *ZThK*, 65 (1968), 398-400.
[25] *Das AT als Buch der Kirche*, p. 82.
[26] "The Evaluation and Authority of the OT Texts," *EOTH*, pp.
308-313.
[27] Pp. 293-299.
[28] P. 313.
[29] *The Christian Faith* (2 vols.; New York, 1963).
[30] *Verheissung*, pp. 75ff.
[31] *Das AT als Buch der Kirche*, pp. 82ff.
[32] Pannenberg, *EOTH*, p. 324.

the NT's method of quotation from the point of view of modern literary criticism.[33] Over against this limited position one must maintain that the NT quotations presuppose the unity of tradition and indicate keywords and major motifs and concepts in order to recall a larger context within the OT.

In direct contrast to the position just described are those attempts that place primary emphasis on the OT by making it all-important theologically. Wilhelm Vischer wants the exegesis of the OT to be dominated by the NT, thereby making the OT all-important.[34] "Strictly speaking only the Old Testament is 'Scripture,' while the New Testament brings the good news that now the content of Scripture — the meaning of all her words, her Lord and her fulfiller has appeared bodily."[35] In very similar terms A. A. van Ruler explains that "the Old Testament is and remains the true Bible."[36] The NT is but "its explanatory glossary [Wörterverzeichnis]."[37] In strict dialectic "The New Testament interprets the Old Testament as well as the Old the New."[38] The central concern in the whole Bible is not reconciliation and redemption but the kingdom of God. For this the OT is of special importance, namely it brings its legitimization, foundation, interpretation, illustration, historicization, and eschatologization.[39] Van Ruler thereby reduces the relationship between the Testaments to the single spiritual denominator of the kingdom of God, reading the NT

[33] Bultmann, *EOTH*, pp. 50-55, 72-75.

[34] *Das Christuszeugnis des AT. Das Gesetz* (7th ed.; Zollikon, 1946); an English translation appeared under the title *The Witness of the OT to Christ* (London, 1949).

[35] *Christuszeugnis*, p. 8. Cf. Schwarzwäller, *EvTh*, 29 (1969), 281-285, for a sympathetic evaluation of Vischer's importance in contemporary theology.

[36] Van Ruler, *The Christian Church and the OT*, p. 72.

[37] P. 74 n. 45.

[38] P. 82.

[39] Pp. 75-98.

very one-sidedly without recognizing the distinction between theocracy and eschatology.[40]

Klaus Schwarzwäller's position should be briefly mentioned here. His thesis is that the OT relates to the NT
in terms of the formula of "course of proof and result."[41]
The OT can be understood only from Christ because it
points forward to him. "The Christ event presupposes
the history of the old covenant and points back into its
testimonies."[42] His position has so far found little
response.

On the whole it must be said that the Christological-
theocratic approaches for the unity of both Testaments
pose special difficulties because they telescope and virtu-
ally eliminate the varieties of the Biblical testimonies.
They suffer from a reductionism of the multiplicity of OT
thought, which merely becomes a pale reflection of the
Messiah to come. Here the somewhat shrill cry of
"Christomonism"[43] has a point. With G. E. Wright, J.
Barr, and R. E. Murphy[44] it seems that the lines of a
Trinitarian approach better meet the needs of delineating the relationship between the Testaments. This approach preserves the *sensus litteralis* of the OT testimony
and avoids the development of a hermeneutical method
based merely on the NT usage of OT texts. Once the
true meaning of Christ is grasped within the context of
the Trinity, then one can say that Christ is the destina-
tion and at the same time the guide to the true understanding of the OT. W. Vischer once posed the question
that remains crucial: "Is the interpretation which reads

[40] A very incisive critique of van Ruler's position has been given by
Th. C. Vriezen, "Theocracy and Soteriology," *EOTH*, pp. 221-223.

[41] *Das AT in Christus*, pp. 51-56.

[42] *EvTh*, 29 (1969), 305.

[43] Wright, *The OT and Theology*, pp. 13-38. He protests against re-
solving the tension between the OT and NT in terms of a "new kind
of monotheism based on Christ" ("Historical Knowledge and Revelation," *Understanding and Translating the OT*, p. 302).

[44] Wright, *Understanding and Translating the OT*, pp. 301-303; Barr,
Old and New in Interpretation, pp. 151-154; Murphy, *Theology Digest*
(1970), 327.

the whole OT as a witness for the Messiah Jesus correct
or does it violate the OT writings?"[45]

A recent major approach to delineate the relationship
between the Testaments is by reverting to typology. W.
Eichrodt[46] and G. von Rad[47] have been staunch supporters. Eichrodt uses typology "as the designation for
a peculiar way of looking at history." The types "are persons, institutions, and events of the Old Testament which
are regarded as divinely established models or prerepre-
sentations of corresponding realities in the New Testament salvation history."[48] His exposition appears to
agree with the traditional views of earlier Christianity.
But he differs from the views of von Rad, whose basic
premise it is that "The Old Testament is a history book."[49]
It is the history of God's people, and the institutions and
prophecies within it, that provide prototypes to the anti-
types of the NT within the whole realm of history and
eschatology.[50] Von Rad is very broadly based, as can be
gathered from his relating Joseph to Christ as type to
antitype.[51]

[45] *Christuszeugnis*, p. 32. Of course, Vischer gives an affirmative
answer to the question. He designates Jesus as the "hidden meaning
of the OT writings" (p. 33). In his book *Die Bedeutung des AT für
das christliche Leben* (Zürich, 1947), p. 5, he writes: "All movements of
life of which the OT reports move from him [Jesus] and towards him.
The life-stories of all these men are part of his life-story. Therefore
they are written with so little biographical interest for the individual
persons. What is written about them is actually written as a part of
the biography of the One through whom and towards whom they live."
This would mean that we can reconstruct a biography of Jesus from
the OT. If Vischer's position were correct it is difficult to perceive why
the OT speaks in the first place about Abraham and Moses. Why does
it not speak right away about Jesus, and why does it speak of him only
in such "hidden" form?

[46] "Is Typological Exegesis an Appropriate Method?" *EOTH*, pp.
224-245.

[47] "Typological Interpretation of the OT," *EOTH*, pp. 17-39; *OTT*,
II, 364-374.

[48] *EOTH*, p. 225.

[49] *EOTH*, p. 25; cf. *OTT*, II, 357.

[50] *OTT*, II, 365.

[51] *OTT*, II, 372.

Some scholars reject the typological approach completely.[52] However, the importance of the typological approach is not to be denied, if it is not developed into a hermeneutic method which is applied to all texts like a divining-rod. Typological correspondence must be rigidly controlled on the basis of direct relationship between various OT elements and their NT counterparts in order that arbitrary and fortuitous personal views may not creep into exegesis.[53] One should be cautious enough not to be trapped into applying typology as *the* single definite theological ground-plan whereby the unity of the Testaments is established. The advocacy of typological unity between the Testaments is not primarily concerned to find a unity of historical facts between the OT prefiguration and its NT counterpart,[54] though this is not to be denied altogether; it is more concerned to recognize the connection in terms of a structural similarity between type and antitype. It is undeniable that the typological analogy begins with a relationship which takes place in history. For example, the typological analogy between Moses and Christ in 2 Cor. 3:7ff. and Heb. 3:1-6 begins with a relationship that takes place in history; but the concern is not with all the details of the life and service of Moses, but primarily with his "ministry"

[52] F. Baumgärtel, *ThLZ*, 86 (1961), 809, 897, 901-906. R. Lucas, "Considerations of Method in OT Hermeneutics," *The Dunwoodie Review*, 6 (1966), 35: "Typology lacks that criterion which would establish both its limitation and validity. . . . It is a theology of biblical texts. It leaves the Old Testament behind, in the last analysis, and discovers its significance outside and beyond its historical testimony." Murphy, *Theology Digest*, 18 (1970), 324, believes that typology is not creative enough for the possibilities of theology and in comparison to the early Church "it is simply less appealing to the modern temper." See also Barr, *Old and New in Interpretation*, pp. 103-148, who is not willing to separate typology from allegory.

[53] See also, with regard to a proper usage of typology, the remarks by H. W. Wolff, "The Hermeneutics of the OT," *EOTH*, pp. 181-186; and Vriezen, *An Outline of OT Theology*², pp. 97, 136f.

[54] Von Rad, however, *EOTH*, pp. 17-19, advocates that the typological approach seeks to "regain reference to the facts attested in the New Testament," i.e., to discover the connection in the historical process.

and "glory" in the former passage and with his "faithfulness" as leader and mediator in the divine dispensation in the second passage. It is equally true that the NT antitype goes beyond the OT type.[55] Even if it is correct, at least to some degree, that the course of history which unites type and antitype emphasizes the distinction between them, while the connection is primarily discovered in its structural analogy and correspondence, this should not be used as an argument against typology unless typology is seen only in terms of a historical process.[56] The conceptual means of the typological correspondence has its distinct place in its expression of the qualification of the Christ-event, but it is in itself not able to express fully the Christ-event in terms of OT history. Therefore additional approaches will need to complement the typological one. The Bible is too rich in relations between God and man for it to be confined to one special connection. Whereas we must not hesitate to accept typological references in definite cases, every attempt to view the whole from a single point of view must beware of wishing to explain every detail in terms of this one aspect and to impose an overall picture upon the variety of possible relations. While the OT context must be preserved in its prefiguration so that NT meanings are not read into the OT texts, it seems that a clear NT indica-

[55] Eichrodt, *EOTH*, pp. 225f.

[56] This is where Pannenberg, *EOTH*, p. 327, goes astray. For him the only analogy that has any value is the historical one. Pannenberg adopts the "promise and fulfillment" schema without realizing that this "structure" (p. 325), as he repeatedly calls it, functions in his own presentation as another instance of a timeless principle being employed to replace history. Pannenberg emphasizes that freeness, creativeness, and unpredictability are central in history, but he finds this central aspect of history preserved only in that the fulfillment often involves the "breaking down" of the prophecy as a "legitimate interpretation," a "transformation of the content of prophecy," which is "fulfilled otherwise" than the original recipients of the prophetic word expected (p. 326). Here Pannenberg has unconsciously conceded the incompatibility between history and its structure. Thus even in Pannenberg's position, structure and construction tend to replace history and render his use of the promise-fulfillment structure unhistorical.

tion is necessary so that subjective imaginative fancies and arbitrary typological analogies can be avoided. That is to say that the question of the *a posteriori* character of the typological approach should not be suppressed.

A prominent approach for coming to grips with the extremely complex question of the relationship between the OT and NT is by way of the promise-fulfillment schema, as developed by C. Westermann, W. Zimmerli, G. von Rad and others.[57] This approach maintains that the OT contains a "history of promise which comes to fruition in the NT."[58] This does *not* mean that the OT describes what was promised and the NT what has been fulfilled.[59] The OT already knows promise and fulfillment. W. Zimmerli makes the point that the promise, when it receives the character of fulfillment in history through Yahweh's guidance and word, receives again a new character of promise.[60] In this way the fulfillment has an open end, looking on to the future.[61] This eschatological aspect is present in both Testaments. Westermann remarks: "Promise and fulfillment constitute an integral event which is reported in both the Old and New Testaments of the Bible." In view of the multiplex character of the relationship between the Testaments,

[57] C. Westermann, "The Way of Promise through the OT," *OTCF*, pp. 200-224; *The OT and Jesus Christ* (Minneapolis, 1970); W. Zimmerli, "Promise and Fulfillment," *EOTH*, pp. 89-122; G. von Rad, "Verheissung," *EvTh*, 13 (1953), 406-413; R. E. Murphy, "The Relationship Between the Testaments," *CBQ*, 26 (1964), 349-359; "Christian Understanding of the OT," *Theology Digest*, 18 (1970), 321-332.

[58] Murphy, *Theology Digest*, 18 (1970), 328.

[59] This is obviously the way in which Fohrer, *ThZ*, 24 (1968), 171f., understands the category of promise-fulfillment. If this mistake is avoided, then there is no conflict between the promise-fulfillment category and Fohrer's beginning-continuation category. Both formulae essentially agree but place emphasis on slightly different aspects.

[60] "Promise and Fulfillment," *EOTH*, p. 112.

[61] This tension between promise and fulfillment is a dynamic characteristic of the OT. Since this is a basic kind of interpreted history which the OT and NT themselves present to us, J. M. Robinson's attempt (*OTCF*, p. 129) to dismiss the category of promise-fulfillment as a structure imposed on Biblical history from without is abortive.

Westermann admits that under the single idea of promise-fulfillment "it is not possible to sum up everything in the relation of the Old Testament to Christ."[62] On a more comprehensive scale, we must admit that the promise-fulfillment schema does not sum up everything in the relation between the Testaments. As fundamental and fruitful as the promise-fulfillment approach is, it is not by itself able to describe the multiplex nature of the relationship between the Testaments.

If we raise the question how the OT can be related adequately and properly to the NT, then we have admittedly decided on an *a priori* basis that both are related to each other in some way. We must be conscious of this decision, which always has a bearing on our questioning of the OT materials. This prior decision does not come easy. This is true especially when the OT is viewed in the way in which von Rad looks at it, namely that "the Old Testament can only be read as a book of ever increasing anticipation."[63] This claim presupposes a particular understanding of the OT history of tradition, that is, one which is from the beginning focusing upon the transition to the NT. Von Rad's view finds its justification only in terms of a direct line of connection that moves from the testimony of the initial action of God toward judgment and on to the expectation of God's renewed action in which God yet proves his divine character. It is amazing to see how Israel never allowed a promise to come to nothing, how she thus swelled Yahweh's promise to an infinity, and how, placing absolutely no limit on God's power yet to fulfill, she transmitted the promises still unfulfilled to generations to come. Thus we must ask with von Rad, "does not the way in which comparative religion takes hold of the Old Testament in abstraction, as an object which can be adequately interpreted without reference to the New Testament, turn out

[62] *The OT and Jesus Christ,* p. 78.
[63] *TAT,* II, 331; *OTT,* II, 319.

to be fictitious from the Christian point of view?"[64] On
the other hand, there is nothing mysterious about coming
to grips with the question of the relationship between
the Testaments. Initially, therefore, we do not begin
from the NT and its manifold references to the OT. This
method has often been adopted, most recently again by
B. S. Childs as we have noted above. It has also led all
too often to contrasting the Testaments with a sharp-
ness that does not do justice to the great hermeneutical
flexibility of the relationship between them. A proper
method will then initially be an attempt to show characteristic ways in which the OT leads forward to the NT.
The NT can then on the basis of this initial approach
also enlighten the content of the OT.

In view of these considerations, it would seem that the
only adequate way to come to grips with the multiplex
nature of the relationship between the Testaments is to
opt for a multiplex approach, which makes a guarded
and circumspect use of typology, employs the idea of
promise-fulfillment, and also uses in a careful way the
approach of *Heilsgeschichte*.[65] Such a multiplex approach leaves room for indicating the variety of connections between the Testaments and avoids, at the same
time, the temptation to explain the manifold testimonies
in every detail by one single point of view or approach
and so to impose a single structure upon testimonies that
witness to something else. A multiplex approach will lead
to a recognition of similarity and dissimilarity, old and
new, continuity and discontinuity, etc., without in the
least distorting the original historical witness and literal

[64] *TAT*, II, 333; *OTT*, II, 321.

[65] We cannot go into the manifold ramifications of the salvation history approach, its weak and strong points as well as its varied use among
past and present theologians. Yet this approach should not be dis-
missed too easily. For a recent exposition of this approach, see O. Cullmann, *Salvation in History* (New York, 1967). A critique is given by D.
Braun, "Heil als Geschichte," *EvTh*, 27 (1967), 57-76. See also the ap-
preciative evaluation of this approach by Kraus, *Die Biblische Theologie*, pp. 185-187.

sense nor falling short in the larger kerygmatic intention
and context to which the OT itself testifies.

It is not suprising that in the recent debate about the
complex nature of the relationship between the Testaments the question of the proper context has become
crucial. Von Rad himself speaks of "the larger context
to which a specific Old Testament phenomenon belongs. . . ."[66] He reflects the concern of H. W. Wolff, who
maintains that "in the New Testament is found the context of the Old, which, as its historical goal, reveals the
total meaning of the Old Testament. . . ."[67] The systematic theologian Hermann Diem expresses himself to the
extent that "for the modern interpretation of Scripture
it can be no question needing judgment whether the
interpretation will follow the apostolic witness and read
the OT with their eyes or whether it will read presup-
positionless, which would mean to read it as a phenomenon of general history of religion. . . ."[68] In a similar
vein Kurt Frör maintains that "the canon forms the given
and compulsory context for all single texts and single
books of both Testaments."[69] The idea of "context"
should not be limited to the nearest relationship of a
pericope, not even to the connection within a book or
historical work. With regard to the larger connections
the canon as a given fact receives hermeneutic relevance.
"The first step on the path of the continuation of the
self-interpretation of the text is to give ear to the remaining Scriptural witnesses."[70] Hans-Joachim Kraus has
sensed what Eichrodt meant when the latter emphasized
that "only where this two-way relationship between the
Old and New Testaments is understood do we find a
correct definition of the problem of OT theology and of

[66] *OTT*, II, 369.
[67] *EOTH*, p. 181.
[68] H. Diem, *Theologie als kirchliche Wissenschaft* (Gütersloh, 1951),
I, 75; cf. his *Was heisst schriftgemäss?* (Gütersloh, 1958), pp. 38f.
[69] *Biblische Hermeneutik* (3rd ed.; München, 1967), p. 65.
[70] Diem, *Was heisst schriftgemäss?* p. 38.

the method by which it is possible to solve it."[71] As regards Kraus his assessment of the matter of the context shows that "the question of the *context* is decisive for the connection of texts and themes. This means for the OT undertaking of Biblical-theological exegesis: How do the Old and New Testaments refer to certain kerygmatic intentions apparent in a text?"[72]

In this connection it is of great importance to explicate what it means that OT theology—and also NT theology—is bound to the given connections of the texts in the canon. Alfred Jepsen writes "that the interpretation of the Old Testament, being the interpretation of the church's canon, is determined by its connection with the New Testament and by the questions that follow from it."[73] If properly conceived, no violence is done to the message of the OT, for what the interpreter receives from the side of the NT is primarily the question, the point of view. To have the right question means to be able to find the right answers. This approach is not a return to a new type of Biblicism. Rather we need to emphasize strongly that Biblical events and meanings must not be looked for behind, beneath, or above the texts,[74] but *in* the texts, because the divine deeds and words have received form and found expression in them. Biblical-theological interpretation attempts to study a passage within its own original historical context, the *Sitz im Leben* of the situation into which a word was spoken or an action took place, and also the life-settings and contextual relations and connections in the later traditions as well as the *Sitz im Leben* in the given context of the book in which it is preserved and the larger

[71] Eichrodt, *TOT,* I, 26.
[72] Kraus, *Die Biblische Theologie,* p. 381 (italics his).
[73] "The Scientific Study of the OT," *EOTH,* p. 265.
[74] This is the way in which Hesse, *Kerygma und Dogma,* IV (1958), 13, seeks to secure a reality that he feels is not there. F. Mildenberger, *Gottes Tat im Wort* (Gütersloh, 1964), pp. 93ff., argues for the unity of the canon as a rule of understanding but revives a new kind of pneumatic exegesis.

kerygmatic intention. In all of this the given context of both Testaments has a bearing on interpretation.[75] Thus the matter of the given context in the nearest and more removed relationships within both Testaments will always have a decisive bearing for Biblical-theological interpretation and for the Biblical theologian's task of doing OT theology. In short, a proper and integral approach to delineating the relationship between the Testaments is cognizant of the meaning and function of context for Biblical-theological interpretation and makes a guarded and circumspect use of typology, the idea of promise-fulfillment, and salvation history.[76] Each of the three latter approaches must be seen as complementing each other rather than being in competition.

[75] Childs, *Biblical Theology in Crisis*, pp. 99ff., has developed the relevance of the "larger canonical context" as the appropriate horizon for Biblical theology and applied it to his own methodological approach. His attempt, however, falls short on account of his establishing a new kind of *dicta probantia* method for doing OT theology on the basis of NT quotations.

[76] Despite von Rad's emphasis on a charismatic-kerygmatic interpretation, his approach goes along the lines of *Heilsgeschichte*. Von Rad's emphasis on typology (*OTT*, II, 323ff.) presupposes a wider salvation-historical framework and connects two points on this background, as is true of the current revival of typological interpretation. On the relationship between typology and salvation history see Cullmann, *Salvation in History*, pp. 132-135. G. Fohrer's negative reaction against the notion of salvation history ("Prophetie und Geschichte," *ThLZ*, 89 [1964], 481ff.) comes on the basis that both salvation and doom are part of salvation history. To a great extent the history of salvation is a history of disaster. Yet even here the continuity is preserved in that later the proclamation of salvation is taken up without the preaching of the message of judgment disappearing. Fohrer's thesis, that the aim of God's action is the rule of God over the world and nature, is not opposed to salvation history but a characteristic part of it.

V. Basic Proposals for Doing OT Theology

Our attempt to focus on unresolved crucial problems which are at the center of the current crisis in OT theology has revealed that there are basic inadequacies in the current methodologies and approaches. The inevitable question that has arisen is, Where do we go from here? Our strictures with regard to the paths trodden by Biblical theologians have indicated that a basically new approach must be worked out. A productive way to proceed from here on appears to have to rest upon the following basic proposals for doing OT theology.

(1) Biblical theology must be understood to be a historical-theological discipline. This is to say that the Biblical theologian engaged in doing either Old or New Testament theology must claim as his task both to discover and describe what the text meant and also to explicate what it means for today. The Biblical theologian attempts to "get back there,"[1] i.e., he wants to do away with the temporal gap by bridging the time span between his day and that of the Biblical witnesses, by means of the historical study of the Biblical documents. The nature of the Biblical documents, however, inasmuch as they are themselves witnesses of the eternal purpose of God for Israel and for the world as mani-

[1] This phrase comes from G. E. Wright, "The Theological Study of the Bible," *The Interpreter's One-Volume Commentary on the Bible* (Nashville, 1971), p. 983.

fested through divine acts and words of judgment and salvation in history, requires a movement from the level of the historical investigation of the Bible to the theological one. The Biblical witnesses are themselves not only historical witnesses in the sense that they originated at particular times and particular places; they are at the same time theological witnesses in the sense that they testify as the word of God to the divine reality and activity as it impinges on the historicality of man. Thus the task of the Biblical theologian is to interpret the Scriptures meaningfully, with the careful use of the tools of historical and philological research, attempting to understand and describe in "getting back there" what the Biblical testimony meant; and to explicate the meaning of the Biblical testimony for modern man in his own particular historical situation.

The Biblical theologian neither takes the place of nor competes with the systematic theologian or dogmatician. The latter has and always will have to fulfill his own task in that he endeavors to use current philosophies as the basis for his primary categories or themes. For the systematic theologian it is indeed appropriate to operate with philosophical categories, because his foundations are on a base different from that of the Biblical theologian. The Biblical theologian draws his categories, themes, motifs, and concepts from the Biblical text itself. The Biblical theologian stands in danger of surreptitiously introducing contemporary philosophy into his discipline.[2] But he must carefully guard himself against this temptation. Therefore, it must be emphasized that the Biblical and systematic theologians do not compete with

[2] A. Dulles (*The Bible in Modern Scholarship*, p. 215) states not incorrectly that "any number of supposedly biblical theologies in our day are so heavily infected with contemporary personalist, existential, or historical thinking as to render their biblical basis highly suspect." In this respect Karl Barth and Rudolf Bultmann have often been accused of finding too many of their own favorite philosophical ideas in the Scriptures.

each other. Their function is complementary. Both need to work side by side, profiting from each other. The Biblical theologian is to present the Biblical categories, themes, motifs, and concepts, which in contrast to the "clear and distinct ideas" of the systematic theologian are often less clear and distinct. All too often the Biblical categories are more suggestive and dynamic ones for expressing the rich revelation of the deep mystery of God. As a result Biblical theology is able to say something to modern man that systematic theology cannot say, and vice versa.

(2) If Biblical theology is understood to be a historical-theological discipline, it follows that its proper method must be both historical *and* theological from the starting-point. A theology of the OT presupposes exegesis based upon sound principles and procedures. Exegesis, in turn, is in need of OT theology. Without OT theology the work of exegetical interpretation may easily become endangered by isolating individual texts from the whole. For example, if one is on the basis of OT theology acquainted with the motif of the remnant in the period prior to and contemporary with the writing prophets, one will not overlook that Amos' use of the remnant motif is to some extent one-sided among the pre-exilic prophets. And if one knows Amos' remnant theology, one will not likely misunderstand the remnant theology as a whole merely as an expression of the positive aspect of a holy remnant saved from eschatological judgment or as an expression of an insignificant and meaningless remainder of God's chosen people.[2a] On the other hand, a careful, clear-sighted, and sound exegesis will always be able to check critically OT theology.

At this point we must pause to note H.-J. Kraus' reminder that "one of the most difficult questions con-

[2a] See the writer's monograph, *The Remnant. The History and Theology of the Remnant Idea from Genesis to Isaiah* (Andrews University Monographs, V; Berrien Springs, Mich., 1972), pp. 173-371.

fronting Biblical theology today is that of the starting-point, the meaning and function of historical-critical research."[3] Von Rad has sensed more keenly than his predecessors who produced OT theologies in this century that the Biblical theologian cannot move on the pathway of a "critically assured minimum," if he actually attempts to grasp "the layers of depth of historical experience, which historical-critical research is unable to fathom."[4] The reason for the inability of the historical-critical method to grasp all layers of depth of historical experience, i.e., the inner unity of happening and meaning based upon the inbreaking of transcendence into history as *the* final reality to which the Biblical text testifies, rests upon its limitation to study history on the basis of its own presuppositions.

The historical-critical method, which came out of the Enlightenment,[5] views history as a closed continuum, an unbroken series of causes and effects in which there is

[3] Kraus, *Die Biblische Theologie*, p. 363; cf. p. 377. On this point Childs (*Biblical Theology in Crisis*, pp. 141f.) writes: "The historico-critical method is an inadequate method for studying the Bible as the Scriptures of the church because it does not work from the needed context. . . . When seen from the context of the canon both the question of what the text meant and what it means are inseparably linked and both belong to the task of interpretation of the Bible as Scripture. To the extent that the use of the critical method sets up an iron curtain between the past and the present, it is an inadequate method for studying the Bible as the church's Scripture." For the inadequacy of the historical-critical method with regard to the new quest of the historical Jesus, see G. E. Ladd, "The Search for Perspective," *Interpretation*, 26 (1971), 41-62.

[4] *TAT*, I, 120; cf. *OTT*, I, 108.

[5] This must be clearly seen, if one does not want to confuse the issues. Ebeling, *Word and Faith*, p. 42: "The critical historical method first arose out of the intellectual revolution of modern times." On this whole point see U. Wilckens, "Über die Bedeutung historischer Kritik in der modernen Bibelexegese," *Was heisst Auslegung der Heiligen Schrift?* (Regensburg, 1966), pp. 85-133. A critique of the adequacy of the historical-critical method for theological research is provided by E. Reisner, "Hermeneutik und historische Vernunft," *ZThK*, 49 (1952), 223-238, and a defense by E. Käsemann, "Vom theologischen Recht historisch-kritischer Exegese," *ZThK*, 64 (1967), 259-281; *Der Ruf der Freiheit* (3rd ed.; München, 1968).

no room for transcendence.[6] "The historian cannot presuppose supernatural intervention in the causal nexus as the basis for his work."[7]

Accordingly, historical events must be capable of being explained by antecedent historical causes and understood in terms of analogy to other historical experiences. The method which prides itself of its scientific nature and objectivity, turns out to be in the grip of its own dogmatic presuppositions and philosophical premises about the nature of history. C. E. Braaten sees the problem as follows: "The historian often begins by claiming that he conducts his research purely objectively, without presuppositions, and ends by surreptitiously introducing a set of presuppositions whose roots lie deeply embedded in an anti-Christian *Weltanschauung*."[8] A Biblical theology which rests upon a view of history that is based on an unbroken continuum of causes and effects cannot do justice to the Biblical view of history and revelation nor to the Scripture's claim to truth.[9] Von Rad has come to recognize that "a consistently applied historico-critical method could [not] really do justice to the Old Testament scripture's claim to truth."[10] What needs to be emphatically stressed is that there is a transcendent or divine dimension in Biblical history which the historical-critical method is unable to deal with. "If all historical

---

[6] *OTT*, II, 418: "For Israel, history consisted only of Jahweh's self-revelation by word and action. And on this point conflict with the modern view of history was sooner or later inevitable, for the latter finds it perfectly possible to construct a picture of history without God. It finds it very hard to assume that there is divine action in history. God has no natural place in its schema."

[7] R. W. Funk, "The Hermeneutical Problem and Historical Criticism," *The New Hermeneutic*, ed. J. M. Robinson and J. B. Cobb, Jr. (New York, 1964), p. 185.

[8] C. E. Braaten, "Revelation, History, and Faith in Martin Kähler," in M. Kähler, *The So-called Historical Jesus and the Historic Biblical Christ* (Philadelphia, 1964), p. 22.

[9] Wallace, *ThZ*, 19 (1963), 90; cf. J. Barr, "Revelation through History in the OT and in Modern Theology," *Interpretation*, 17 (1963), 201f.

[10] *OTT*, II, 417.

events must by definition be explained by sufficient historical causes, then there is no room for the acts of God
in history, for God is not a historical character."[11] If one's
view of history is such that one cannot acknowledge a
divine intervention in history through deed and word,
then one is unable to deal adequately and properly with
the testimony of Scripture. We are, therefore, led to con-
clude that the crisis respecting history in Biblical theology is not so much a result of the scientific study of the
evidences, but stems from the historical-critical method's
inadequacy to deal with the role of transcendence in history due to its philosophical presuppositions about the
nature of history.[12] If the reality of the Biblical text testifies to a supra-historical dimension which transcends the
self-imposed limitations of the historical-critical method,
then one must employ a method that can account for
this dimension and can probe into all the layers of depth
of historical experience and deal adequately and properly
with the Scripture's claim to truth.[13]

We have stated that the proper method for Biblical
theology is to be both historical *and* theological from the
beginning. Too often it is assumed that exegesis has the
historical-critical function to work out the meaning of
single texts, and Biblical theology the task to join these
single aspects into a theological *whole*, namely a sequential procedure. H.-J. Kraus has rightly called for a "Biblical-theological process of interpretation" in which exegesis is from its starting-point Biblical-theological in

---

[11] Ladd, *Interpretation*, 26 (1971), 50.

[12] Von Rad, *TAT*, II, 9: "Die historische Methode eröffnet uns nur
einen Aspekt in das vielschichtige Phänomen der Geschichte und zwar
einen, der über das Verhältnis der Geschichte zu Gott schlechterdings
nichts auszusagen vermag."

[13] Von Rad, *TAT*, I, 120; *OTT*, I, 108. Osswald, *Wissenschaftliche
Zeitschrift der Universität Jena,* 14 (1965), 711: "Mit Hilfe der kritischen
Wissenschaft kann freilich keine Aussage über Gott gemacht werden,
denn es führt kein Weg von der objektivierenden Geschichtswissen-
schaft zur eigentlichen theologischen Aussage. Das verstandesmässige
Erkennen der Geschichte bleibt auf die raum-zeitliche Dimension be-
schränkt. . . ."

orientation.[14] If we add to this aspect that a proper and adequate method of research dealing with the Biblical text needs to take into account the reality of God and his inbreaking into history,[15] because the Biblical text testifies to the transcendent dimension in historical reality,[16] then we have a basis upon which historical *and* theological interpretation can go hand in hand from the start without needing to be artificially separated into sequential processes.[17] On this basis one is able to "get back there" into the world of the Biblical writer by bridging the temporal and cultural gap, and can attempt to understand historically and theologically what the text meant. It is then possible to express more adequately and comprehensively what the text means for man in the modern world and historical situation.

This methodological procedure does not seek to skip

[14]*Die Biblische Theologie,* p. 377.

[15] This point is also made by Floyd V. Filson, "How I Interpret the Bible," *Interpretation,* 4 (1950), 186: "I work with the conviction that the only really objective method of study takes the reality of God and his working into account, and that any other point of view is loaded with presuppositions which actually, even if subtly, contain an implicit denial of the full Christian faith."

[16] One presupposition of the historical-critical method is the consistent application of the principle of analogy. E. Tröltsch writes, "The means by which criticism [with the historical-critical method] is at all possible is the application of analogy. . . . But the omnipotence of analogy implies that all historical events are identical in principle" (quoted by von Rad, *OTT,* I, 107). Von Rad states in *TAT,* II, 9, that also the course of history as built up by the historical-critical method "is interpreted history on the basis of historical-philosophical presuppositions, which do not allow any possible recognition of God's action in history, because only man is notoriously considered to be the creator of history." Mildenberger, *Gottes Tat im Wort,* p. 31 n. 37, agrees with von Rad and adds that historical criticism "presupposes a closed relation of reality which cannot grant 'supernatural' causes."

[17] On this point von Rad, *TAT,* II, 12, has made the following observation: "Die theologische Deutung der alttestamentlichen Texte setzt aber nicht erst da ein, wo der literarkritisch und historisch geschulte Exegete (so oder so!) seine Arbeit getan hat, so dass wir also zwei Arbeitsgänge hätten, einen historisch-kritischen und dann einen 'theologischen.' Die theologische Deutung, die in dem Text eine Aussage von Gott zu begreifen sucht, ist vom ersten Anfang des Verstehungsprozesses wirksam."

history in favor of theology. The Biblical theologian working with the method that is both historical and theological recognizes fully the relativity of human objectivity.[18] Accordingly he is aware that he must never let his faith cause him to modernize his materials on the basis of the tradition and community of faith in which he stands. He must ask questions of the Biblical text on its own terms; he makes room that his tradition and the content of his faith may be challenged, guided, enlivened, and enriched by his finds. He recognizes also that a purely philological, linguistic, and historical approach is never enough to disclose the full and complete meaning of a historical text. One can apply all the exegetical instruments available from historical, linguistic, and philological research and never reach the heart of the matter unless one yields to the basic experience out of which the Biblical writers speak, namely faith. Without so yielding, one will never come to a recognition of the full reality that finds expression in the Biblical testimony. We do not wish to turn faith into a method, nor do we intend to disregard the demand of the Biblical books, as documents from the past, to translate them as objectively as possible by careful employment of the respective and proper methods of interpretation. But we mean that the interpretation of Scripture is to become part of our own real experience, as should all interpretation.[19] The historical-theological interpretation is to be at the service of faith, if it is to fathom all layers of depth of historical experience and to penetrate into the full meaning of the text and the reality expressed in it. We must, therefore, affirm that when interpretation seeks to grasp statements and

[18] So also Stendahl, *IDB,* I, 422.

[19] To confine oneself to philology, linguistics, and history when studying the Gilgamesh Epic or the Assyrian annals, without ever giving oneself over to the thought of the authors of these documents, without ever trying to share in the experiences of the authors that came to expression in these documents, would mean to miss forever the concept of reality which these men discovered and which made up their very life and thought.

testimonies witnessing to God's self-disclosure as the Lord of time and event, who had chosen to reveal himself in actual datable happenings of human history through acts and words of judgment and salvation, then the process of understanding such statements and testimonies must be from the start both historical *and* theological in nature in order to comprehend fully the complete reality that has come to expression.

(3) The Biblical theologian engaged in OT theology has his subject indicated beforehand inasmuch as his endeavor is a theology of the *Old* Testament. It is founded exclusively on materials taken from the OT. The OT comes to him through the Christian church as part of the inspired Scriptures. Introduction to the OT seeks to throw light on the pre-literary and literary stages and forms of the OT books by tracing their history of transmission and formation as well as the text-forms and the canonization of the OT. The history of Israel is studied in the context of the history of antiquity with special emphasis on the ancient Near East, where archeology has been invaluable in providing the historical, cultural, and social setting for the Bible. Exegesis has the task to disclose the full meaning of the individual texts.

Old Testament theology questions the various books or blocks of writings of the OT as to their theology.[20] For the OT is composed of writings whose origin, content, forms, intentions, and meaning are very diverse. The nature of these matters makes it imperative to look at the material at hand in light of the context which is primary to us, namely the form in which we meet it first, as a verbal structure of an integral part of a

[20] This has been stressed for NT theology especially by Heinrich Schlier ("The Meaning and Function of a Theology of the NT," *Dogmatic vs. Biblical Theology*, ed. H. Vorgrimler [Baltimore, 1964], pp. 88-90); for OT theology by Kraus (*Die Biblische Theologie*, p. 364), by D. J. McCarthy ("The Theology of Leadership in Joshua 1-9," *Biblica*, 52 [1971], 166), and with his own emphasis by Childs (*Biblical Theology in Crisis*, pp. 99-107).

literary whole.[21] Viewed in this way an OT theology will neither become a "history of religion,"[22] "history of the transmission of tradition," or "history of revelation,"[23] nor will it turn into a "theology of redaction criticism" or something of that sort. A theology of the OT is first of all a summary interpretation and explanation of the OT writings or blocks of writings. This does not imply that there is no value in capturing the theology of particular traditions; it simply views this to be part of another endeavor. The procedure of explicating the theology of the OT books or blocks of writing in the final form as verbal structures of literary wholes has the distinct advantage

[21] Contemporary (non-Biblical) literary critics place special emphasis upon the "new criticism," which the Germans call *Werkinterpretation*. Cf. W. Kayser, *Das sprachliche Kunstwerk* (10th ed.; Bern-München, 1964); Emil Staiger, *Die Kunst der Interpretation* (4th ed.; Zürich, 1963); Horst Enders, ed., *Die Werkinterpretation* (Darmstadt, 1967). The primary concern according to the practitioners of the "new criticism" is to occupy oneself with the study of a finished piece of literature. The "new criticism" insists on the formal integrity of the literary piece as a work of art, the *Kunstwerk*. Such a work must be appreciated in its totality; to look behind it in an attempt at discovering its history of origin is irrelevant. The emphasis is on the finished literary product *qua* work of art. An increasing number of OT scholars have taken up the emphasis of the "new criticism." Among them are: Z. Adar, *The Biblical Narrative* (Jerusalem, 1959); S. Talmon, " 'Wisdom' in the Book of Esther," *VT*, 13 (1963), 419-455; M. Weiss, "Wege der neueren Dichtungswissenschaft in ihrer Anwendung auf die Psalmenforschung," *Biblica*, 42 (1961), 225-302; "Einiges über die Bauformen des Erzählens in der Bibel," *VT*, 13 (1963), 455-475; "Weiteres über die Bauformen des Erzählens in der Bibel," *Biblica*, 46 (1965), 181-206.

[22] One should refrain from designating a book like H. Ringgren's *Israelite Religion* (Philadelphia, 1966) as an OT theology. Ringgren himself states that "the reader will not find in this book a theology of the Old Testament but a history of Israelite religion. . . . Theologians will also miss points of view based on *Heilsgeschichte;* these points of view have their place, but only within a theological presentation" (p. v).

[23] Kraus, *Die Biblische Theologie,* p. 365: " 'Biblical theology' should be *biblical* theology in that it accepts the canon in the given textual connections as *the historical truth* which is in need of explanation, whose final form is in need of being presented by interpretation and summary. This should be the actual task of Biblical theology. Every attempt at a different procedure would not be Biblical theology, but 'history of revelation,' 'history of religion,' or even 'history of tradition' " (italics his).

of recognizing the similarities *and* differences between the various books or blocks of writings. This means for example that the theologies of the individual prophetic writings will be able to stand independently next to each other. Each voice can be heard in its testimony to the activity of God and the divine self-disclosure. Another advantage of this approach, one that is crucial for the whole enterprise of OT theology, is that no systematic scheme, pattern of thought, or extrapolated abstraction is superimposed upon the Biblical materials. Since no single theme, scheme, or motif is sufficiently comprehensive to include within it all varieties of OT viewpoints, one must refrain from using a particular concept, formula, basic idea, etc., as the center of the OT whereby a systematization of the manifold and variegated OT testimonies is achieved. On the other hand, we must affirm that God is the center of the OT as its central subject. By saying that God is the center of the OT we have stated that the OT Scripture has a central content without falling into the trap of organizing the event-centered character and manner of God's self-disclosing revelation into a system. It is refraining to systematize that which cannot be systematized without losing its essential nature.

(4) The presentation of the theologies of the OT books, or groups of writings, will preferably not follow the order of the books in the canonical sequence, for this order, whether in the Hebrew canon or the LXX, etc., had apparently other than theological causes. Though admittedly difficult to fix, the date of origin of the books, groups of writings, or blocks of material within these writings may provide a guide for establishing the order of presentation of the various theologies.

(5) An OT theology not only seeks to know the theology of the various books, or groups of writings; it also attempts to draw together and present the major themes of the OT. To live up to its name, OT theology must al-

low its themes, motifs, and concepts to be formed for it
by the OT itself. The range of OT themes, motifs, and
concepts will always impose itself on the theologian insofar as they silence his own, once the theological perspectives of the OT are really grasped. On principle, a
theology of the OT must tend toward themes, motifs,
and concepts and must be presented with all the variety
and all the limitations imposed on them by the OT itself.

For example, the election themes as reflected in God's
call to Abraham and his promises to him and the fathers
of Israel, God's deliverance of enslaved Israel in the
exodus experience with Israel's establishment in the
Promised Land, and God's choice of and promises to
David with Zion/Jerusalem as the holy mountain and
divine dwelling-place, are in need of being presented in
an OT theology in their variety of appearances and us-
ages in the individual books or blocks of material. This
would be equally true with regard to so central a concept as the Mosaic covenant. The utterly gracious action
of the Giver of the covenant drew from the recipients a
response, and created the special and unique relationship between them and their God. The covenant concept furnishes major elements for worship and cult as
well as for the proclamation of the prophets and the
theology of the historical books. Inherent in these and
other OT concepts, motifs, and themes is a basic future
expectation, viz., the outstanding blessing for all nations,
the new Exodus, the second David, the new Jerusalem,
the new covenant, which reveals that Israelite faith needs
to be viewed as intensely directed toward the future.
Special motifs in the wisdom theology stress man's life
and responsibility in the here and now. It is beyond our
purpose to list the variety of major concepts, themes,
and motifs.

The presentation of these longitudinal perspectives of
the OT testimonies can be achieved only on the basis of
a multitrack treatment. The richness of the OT testi-

monies can be grasped by such a multiplex approach as is commensurate with the nature of the OT. This multiplex approach with the multitrack treatment of longitudinal themes frees the Biblical theologian from the notion of an artificial and forced unilinear approach determined by a single structuring concept, whether it is covenant, communion, kingdom of God, or something else, to which all OT testimonies, thoughts, and concepts are made to refer or are forced to fit.

(6) As the OT is interrogated for its theology, it answers first of all by yielding various theologies, namely those of the individual books and groups of writings, and then by yielding the theologies of the various longitudinal themes. But the name of our discipline as *theology* of the OT is not only concerned to present and explicate the variety of different theologies. The concept foreshadowed by the name of the discipline has *one* theology in view, namely *the* theology of the OT.

The final aim of OT theology is to demonstrate whether or not there is an inner unity that binds together the various theologies and longitudinal themes, concepts, and motifs. This is an extremely difficult undertaking which contains many dangers. If there is behind the experience of those who left us the OT Scriptures a unique divine reality, then it would seem that behind all variegation and diversity of theological reflection there is a hidden inner unity which has also drawn together the OT writings. The ultimate object of a theology is then to draw the hidden inner unity out of its concealment as much as possible and to make it transparent.

The task to achieve this objective must not be performed too hastily. The constant temptation to find unity in a single structuring theme or concept must be avoided. Here misgivings should arise not only because OT theology would be reduced to a cross-sectional or some other development of a single theme or concept, but the real task would be lost sight of, which is precisely not to overlook or pass by the variegated and divers theologies while at the same time to search for and articulate the inner unity which seemingly binds together in a concealed way the divergent and manifold OT testimonies. One can indeed speak of such a unity in which ultimately the divergent theological utterances and testimonies are intrinsically related to each other from the theological viewpoint on the basis of a presupposition that derives from the inspiration and canonicity of the OT as Scripture.

A seemingly successful way to come to grips with the question of unity is to take the various major longitudinal themes and concepts and explicate whether and how the variegated theologies are intrinsically related to each other. In this way the underlying bond of the one theology of the OT may be illuminated. In the quest to find and explicate the inner unity one must refrain from making the theology of one book or group of books the norm of what is OT theology. For example, one must not make a particular theology of history the norm of OT theology.[24] The often neglected theologies, among them especially those of the wisdom materials of the OT, must be allowed to stand side by side with other theologies. They make their own special contributions to OT theology on equal basis with those more recognized ones, because they too are expressions of OT realities. The question of unity implies tension, but tension does not of necessity mean contradiction. It would appear that where conceptual unity seems impossible the creative tension thereby produced will turn out to be a most fruitful one for OT theology.

(7) The Biblical theologian understands OT theology as being more than the "theology of the Hebrew Bible." The name "theology of the Old Testament" implies the

---

[24] This has been the case even in von Rad's approach. He has chosen a particular theology of history, that of the Deuteronomist, as the main norm for his exposition of OT theology. Thus the wisdom traditions are forced to recede into the background.

larger context of the Bible of which the New Testament is the other part. An integral OT theology must demonstrate its basic relationship to the NT or to NT theology. For the Christian theologian the OT has the character of Scripture on the basis of its relation to the other Testament.

As noted earlier, the multiplex question and complex nature of the relationship between the Testaments and its implication for OT theology make it necessary to opt for a multiplex approach, which makes a guarded and circumspect use of typology, employs the idea of promise-fulfillment, and uses also in a careful manner *Heilsgeschichte.* A multiplex approach leaves room for indicating the variety of connections between the Testaments and avoids an explication of the manifold testimonies through a single structure or unilinear point of view. The multiplex approach has the advantage of remaining faithful to both similarity and dissimilarity as well as old and new without in the least distorting the original historical witness of the text in its literal sense and its larger kerygmatic intention nor falling short in the recognition of the larger context to which the OT belongs. Thus both Testaments will finally shed light upon each other and aid mutually in a more comprehensive understanding of their theologies.

✿   ✿   ✿

On the basis of these proposals outlining a new approach to OT theology, one is in a position to work out a theology of the OT that may avoid the pitfalls and blind alleys that have precipitated the current crisis in OT theology. At the same time one may be a crucial step closer in bringing about a much hoped for and talked about Biblical theology of both the Old and New Testaments.

Supplementary Bibliography

The following contributions supply additional background for a more comprehensive understanding of the issues under discussion: C. T. Craig, "Biblical Theology and the Rise of Historicism," *JBL*, 62 (1943), 281-294; F. Filson, "Biblische Theologie in Amerika," *ThLZ*, 75 (1950), 71-80; N. W. Porteous, "OT Theology," in *The OT and Modern Study*, ed. H. H. Rowley (London, 1951), pp. 311-345; C. Spicq, "L'avènement de la théologie biblique," *RScPhTh*, 35 (1951), 561-574; "Nouvelles réflexions sur la théologie biblique," *RScPhTh*, 43 (1958), 209-219; F. M. Braun, "La théologie biblique," *Revue Thomiste*, 61 (1953), 221-253; G. Ebeling, "The Meaning of 'Biblical Theology'," *Journal of Theological Studies*, 6 (1955), 210-225, now in *Word and Faith* (Philadelphia, 1963), pp. 79-97; V. de Leeuw, "Overzicht van de oudtestamentische theologie," *Ex Oriente Lux*, 14 (1955/56), 122-128; H. Gross, "Was ist alttestamentliche Theologie?" *Trierer Theologische Zeitschrift*, 67 (1958), 355-363; R. Martin-Achard, "Les voies de la théologie de l'AT," *Revue de Théologie et de Philosophie*, 3 (1959), 217-226; H. Wildberger, "Auf dem Wege zu einer biblischen Theologie," *EvTh*, 19 (1959), 70-90; J. Lindblom, "Vad innebär en 'teologisk' syn på gamla Testamentet?" *Svensk Teologisk Kvartalskrift*, 37 (1961), 73-91; A. J. Bjørndalen, "Det Gamle Testamentets Teologi, Metodiske hovedproblemer," *Tidsskrift for Teologi og Kirke*, 30 (1959), 92-116; F. Festorazzi, "Rassegna di teologia dell'AT," *Rivista Biblica*, 10 (1962), 297-316; 12 (1964), 27-48; R. C. Dentan, *Preface to OT Theology* (2nd ed.; New York, 1963); Ch. Barth, "Grundprobleme einer Theologie des AT," *EvTh*, 23 (1963), 342-372; D. Wallace, "Biblical Theology: Past and Future," *ThZ*, 19 (1963), 88-105; P. Wernberg-Möller, "Is There an OT Theology?" *Hibbert Journal*, 59 (1960), 21-29; L. Ramlot, "Une décade de théologie biblique," *Revue Thomiste*, 6 (1964), 65-96; 7 (1965), 95-135; R. E. Clements, "The Problem of OT Theology," *London Quarterly and Holborn Review* (Jan. 1965), pp. 11-17; J. Barr, *Old*

and New in Interpretation (New York, 1966), pp. 65-102; H. F.
Hahn, *The OT in Modern Research* (2nd ed.; Philadelphia, 1966),
pp. 226-249, 302-307; R. K. Harrison, *Introduction to the OT*
(Grand Rapids, 1969), pp. 415-491; R. B. Laurin, *Contemporary
OT Theologians* (Valley Forge, Pa., 1970); H.-J. Kraus, *Die Bib-
lische Theologie. Ihre Geschichte und Problematik* (Neukirchen-
Vluyn, 1970); J. Harvey, "The New Diachronic Biblical Theology
of the OT," *Biblical Theology Bulletin,* 1 (1971), 5-29; F. C. Pruss-
ner, "The Covenant of David and the Problem of Unity in OT
Theology," *Transition in Biblical Scholarship,* ed. J. C. Rylaarsdam
(Chicago, 1968), pp. 17-44; W. H. Schmidt, *Das erste Gebot. Seine
Bedeutung für das AT* (München, 1969); R. Davidson, "The The-
ology of the OT," *Biblical Criticism,* ed. R. Davidson and A. R. C.
Leany (London, 1970), pp. 138-165; H. Gese, "Erwägungen zur
Einheit der biblischen Theologie," *ZThK,* 67 (1970), 417-436; H.
W. Wolff, ed. *Probleme biblischer Theologie. Gerhard von Rad
zum 70. Geburtstag* (München, 1971).

Index of Authors

Index of Subjects